YOU ARE THE
CHANGE

A BEGINNER'S GUIDE TO
SOCIALLY RESPONSIBLE INVESTING

By Stephan Kerby

For Keigan and Kaya

The mind is not a vessel that needs filling,

but wood that needs igniting.

Plutarch

CONTENTS

1

WHAT IS SOCIALLY RESPONSIBLE INVESTING?

This book provides a description of Socially Responsible Investing (SRI), explains how it has evolved over the years, and shows how to utilize it in your investment portfolio. The strategies in this book illuminate a roadmap for those who aspire to become responsible investors. Throughout the book, I provide tools and resources for you to use while working with your advisor to incorporate SRI strategies into your portfolio. The following pages introduce the concept of SRI and how it can enable you to both grow your investments and make a meaningful impact at the same time.

I decided to write this book because the other books I had read on the subject were either overly complicated or not comprehensive enough. I wanted to create a clear, balanced guide for average investors who are interested in making socially responsible investing a part of their overall financial plans. This book is also geared toward advisors who want to learn how they can play a role in helping their clients navigate the SRI world effectively.

For the sake of simplicity, I will be using the term "SRI" throughout this book, but what we're calling "Socially Responsible Investing" can go by several different names. Some refer to it as social investment, and it is also known as sustainable, socially conscious, green, or ethical investing. Here is a simple definition of socially responsible investing:

> *Socially responsible investing is any investment strategy that seeks to consider both financial return and social/environmental good to bring about a positive change in society as a whole.*

Later in the book, I will discuss some of the other terms and acronyms used, but for now, we will keep it simple and stick with SRI.

It is important to emphasize that investing must be based on an overall financial plan because typically, investing is not an isolated, one-time occurrence. Other factors and goals can impact your investments, so it is important to have a plan that looks at these potential roadblocks and opportunities. Your goals and plan can change along the way, but you need to have a solid starting point to determine the proper course.

When working with my clients, we take the necessary time to determine the objective of the investment portfolio. We look at everything, including the timeframe, risk tolerance, return objective, tax impact, and even the relation between the new potential investment and the current investment mix. All of this helps us determine the best way to move ahead and create an investment model/portfolio that reflects the client's objectives and risk tolerance. Once you figure out how you should split up your investments with regard to asset classes (asset allocation and diversification[i]), then it becomes about finding the right investments to fill those needs. This process may sound complex initially, but I will break it down in a simple format throughout the book.

To be clear, I recommend that you always consult with a professional before making any investment decisions. This book is not intended or designed to provide specific investment advice or recommendations. It is designed to motivate and encourage you to dig deeper into the subject, and to consider SRI in your specific situation. While this book is addressed to a US audience, the information is relevant globally.

The views expressed in this book are solely my own and do not represent those of any other organizations, advisors at my firm, my broker dealer, or OSJ (Office of Supervisory Jurisdiction). Any references to specific rates, return, or performance of investments are purely historical and do not guarantee future results. SRI, like all investing, involves great risks and potential for loss. Again, I recommend consulting a professional before implementing any ideas you may formulate after reading this book.

2

BACKGROUND

Twenty years ago, I met with someone from my church who was interested in avoiding investments in companies that were involved in certain areas of the market. As a Christian, he did not want to support products and industries that were in conflict with his religious beliefs. This meeting was my first encounter with the concept of SRI, and I have been captivated by this strategy ever since. People from all walks of life have beliefs, personal values, and issues they stand for, but most are unaware that their investment dollars are doing harm to the causes they care about on a daily basis. This realization opened my eyes to new avenues and possibilities.

Most of us are saving—for retirement, for education, or for some other reason. However, few people realize that their investment dollars have not only the potential for growth but also the potential to support companies they believe in while avoiding those they don't. Can you imagine the impact on the world if everyone were to use their voting dollars to support companies that are truly innovative, profitable, and forward-thinking, rather than companies with a purely for-profit motive? What a difference we could make if we educated and encouraged investors to be active shareholders who recognize that they are part-owners and have a voice in the future direction of companies.

I frequently hear people complaining about companies they disapprove of. When I ask them if they are invested in any of these companies, most people will say no. After a pause, however, the initial "no" is often followed by "I don't know," which is the truth for most investors. I see this gap in awareness as an opportunity. The chance encounter twenty years ago with the investor from my church made me realize that many people are already part-owners of these companies, but they are either unaware of it or unsure of how to use that ownership to make an impact. SRI is more than just buying a different type of fund; it's about finding others with the same values and working with companies to help drive real change. It's about being a responsible owner and directly impacting change on the corporate level to benefit society as a whole, rather than passively sitting on the sidelines. It's putting your money where your heart is.

If you have a retirement plan at work or an IRA, you most likely own mutual funds[ii]. A mutual fund is essentially a basket of stocks. So, for example, if you're a vegan and are ethically opposed to purchasing meat, the odds are still extremely high that you are supporting a large producer of pork or chicken through your investments in your retirement program. You are voting for them, and upholding their practices, by investing in their company. The fact that you don't buy steak at the grocery store is of no consequence to these corporations because you are inadvertently supporting them through purchasing their stock. The realization can be challenging, but it is necessary. For me, this became the mission: to help people look into their accounts and determine what companies they do and do not want to fund, based on their values. It is practicing what you preach on an investment level.

Today, twenty years after I first learned about SRI, it is at the forefront of my practice. Demonstrating my commitment to the field, I became the first advisor to achieve the Chartered SRI Counselor™ or CSRIC™ designation through the College of Financial Planning. Since my start in the industry, SRI has changed, evolved, expanded, and improved in many ways. Total US assets under management using SRI strategies grew from $6.57 trillion in 2014 to $8.72 trillion in 2016, which is a 33% increase and accounts for 1 in 5 investment dollars—let that sink in (US SIF 2016). Moreover, since I began work on this book, new data has come out to support my theory that this is not a short-term trend. In 2018, US SIF (The Forum for Sustainable and Responsible Investment, formerly known as the Social Investment Forum) issued its annual trends report and showed a 38% growth in assets using SRI over the previous two years, totaling $12 trillion or 1 in every 4 dollars under professional management (US SIF 2018). So, let's not pretend that this is just a fad. The growth in this sector will continue as we see major demographic shifts, new investment options, expansion of research, and—one of the most impactful events —the largest transfer of wealth (over $30 trillion) currently being passed down to millennials. Surveys show that over 84% of those born between 1981 and 1996 are interested in sustainable and responsible investing. As of 2016, women control or own over half of the wealth in the US and, when surveyed, over 79% said they were interested in socially responsible investing (Natixis Investment Managers 2016).

While this growth is impressive, the US still lags behind much of the world in adopting SRI practices. Other countries lead the way and have integrated environmental, social, and governance (ESG) screening and SRI into many aspects of public and private investments. In 2016, Europe was leading the world with more than 52% of global SRI assets or $11 trillion in investments, and it's growing substantially every year (Medland 2017). The low level of engagement throughout America is a significant issue given that US corporations have much stronger lobbying powers and, due to a lack of transparency, can quietly make destructive decisions without public scrutiny. So, we have some work to do.

From a global perspective, when you observe the trillions of dollars in assets, the multitude of organizations, forums, and researchers who have adopted SRI on such a large scale, it should make you curious. You might wonder, why are some of the largest, wealthiest endowments and organizations from around the world demanding and embracing socially responsible investments? Why are more and more money managers moving towards sustainable investments for their portfolios? Do they know something I don't? The short answer is yes, and as we continue, we will uncover what that is.

With this book, I intend to help you unpack the realization that you can have an impact while saving for retirement or investing for some future goal. It's your adventure—in one version of the story, you're actively exercising constructive influence, and in the other version of the story, you're just another investor going through the motions. I can't choose which story is right for you, but I can provide the tools to help you make that decision for yourself.

It is realistic to achieve investment results that are similar to or better than your current results by using sustainable and socially responsible investing strategies. In addition, you can use your investment dollars to reduce your carbon footprint, keep companies on their toes, and make an impact, all while working toward your financial goals. You're not alone in your fight, whether it be working for environmental justice, prison reform, labor issues, gender equity, or one of many other issues. There are millions just like you, looking to work collaboratively for change. My hope is that you feel empowered to make a change while essentially doing what you're already doing—saving and investing—but with a few adjustments. There are fellow investors from all income levels and all walks of life that share your passion. When we coordinate our investments to vote as a unit, we are powerful. Once you start to see the change taking place, it won't make sense to you to invest any other way.

The beauty of SRI as a strategy is that it transcends all political and religious affiliations and applies to everyone. We each have issues we care about, and we all want to create change, but we might not all agree on how to do that. Some of you may be purely motivated by the belief that SRI can help with risk and return over the long term. Some of you may be more focused on investing with your values, voting with your conscience, or reducing your carbon footprint. Regardless, I welcome you to the game! Just like in a political election, I don't have to agree with your vote—the fact that you're voting is what's important.

As more investors recognize that they are actually owners who can have a say in corporate decision-making, many companies will do everything they can to adjust the rules, moving the bar to hoard as much control as possible. However, as more investors become directly involved, companies will realize that we are watching. They will know we are exercising our right to vote and making sure that their profits are earned sustainably, and not at the cost of society, the environment, or humanity. Together, we can take a major step forward.

SUMMARY

I want this book to be fun and interesting as well as educational, so I will give a brief, casual summary at the end of each chapter, focusing on the most important points to make them easier to digest. Each summary will include ideas for investors, as well as ideas for advisors and other investment professionals.

This book will give you a basic history of socially responsible investing and its evolution, encouraging you to see if it's a fit for you. Unfortunately, few advisors understand SRI and how to utilize it, which means that it is often not mentioned to clients as an option. According to a study conducted by Nuveen, the number of financial advisors who reported speaking with clients about SRI options increased from 18% in 2017 to 33% in 2018. While this growth is encouraging, a huge gap still remains between advisors and the 81% of investors who say they want their investments to work toward improving environmental sustainability. Unsurprisingly, most investors also considered advisors who discuss SRI to be more forward-thinking (Nuveen 2018).

Remember, the term SRI refers to Socially Responsible Investing. This book is designed to encourage investors and advisors to consider SRI. Much of the world has already embraced it for a reason—it's a way you can have your financial cake and eat it too. You can invest towards your goals while making an impact with those same investment dollars. Let me clearly state again that investing should be done as part of a comprehensive financial plan. Without specific goals and assumptions, it's difficult to determine the best allocation, or how to diversify the portfolio. Like all investing, SRI is inherently risky, and you should consult a financial professional, preferably one with the CSRIC™ designation, as they have shown a commitment to expertise in this field.

FOR INVESTORS: I want this book to simplify SRI while assisting you in the exploration of how it can help grow your portfolio. I believe that making this information accessible will help you find your voice for change. You're already investing through your employer or on your own. Just a small change to where you're investing, or whom you're investing with, can have a major impact. There are organizations out there to help you use your mutual funds and stocks to vote and create change, so I want to motivate and encourage you in this area. We need more good people in the fight. I am convinced that if more people understood that they could be voting for change with their investment dollars, they would use them proactively. Sadly, the majority of investors have no idea how to make this happen. It is my mission to change that.

Your investments are a powerful way to use your voice. I hope to show you how to use that voice to facilitate the changes you would like to see in society. By using sustainable and socially responsible investing, you can take your complaints from social media right to the boardroom. You can invest in your future and impact future generations. This process doesn't have to be intimidating or stressful. With this book, I will demystify socially responsible investing and give you a framework to help you understand it.

FOR ADVISORS: As I mentioned, roughly 80% of investors are interested in SRI. As advisors, we are falling short in this area and need more people who are educated on the topic. You can become informed through the College for Financial Planning and the CSRIC™ designation. Also, US SIF has an introductory course on their site where you can learn a bit more. If you have considered SRI in the past, but decided against it, I ask you to reconsider after reading this book. It's likely you will see what I see:

the revolutionary screening of investment information and the potential for positive returns with a positive impact. The data is here to support this area of planning, as the US SIF has reported. With a 38% growth in assets using SRI over the last two years, totaling $12 trillion or 1 in every 4 dollars under professional management, ignoring SRI will mean being left in the dust.

Once you learn about where SRI is today, you can't help but see its value. In addition, you will meet all kinds of awesome, inspirational people while learning about issues you can actually influence. How is that not the dream job? Yes, it's great to be able to help a family save for the future. But when you help a family save for the future, and also reduce their carbon footprint, help promote gender justice, and clean up waterways, you have just exponentially amplified your job! So, to my fellow advisors, I hope this book encourages you to do your own research and verify the information I present. Then, join the movement by helping your clients save money and create change because if you don't, someone else will.

3

SOCIALLY RESPONSIBLE INVESTING TERMS

When people begin digging into the concept of SRI, they usually hit a confusing roadblock of labels and acronyms. As I mentioned earlier, there are many different terms in use to describe this area, but I have chosen to use SRI because it is a broad term. It encompasses the connected ideas of socially astute people who use their investment dollars to effect change. The strategy encourages corporate practices that promote environmental stewardship, diversity, consumer protection, human rights, and animal rights, while manifesting an achievable financial return. To me, the definition is that simple.

ALTERNATIVE TERMS

When I was first starting in this area, SRI simply stood for Socially Responsible Investing, and the origin of most SRI was motivated by religious values. For the most part, it was understood to be an investment strategy based on avoiding industries or companies involved in tobacco, alcohol, pornography, military, and gambling, which are commonly known as "sin stocks."

Although I still use the term "Socially Responsible Investing," the industry has begun a transformation, and there are now several variations of SRI. The term "Sustainable and Responsible Investing" is the updated umbrella term that most in the industry now favor for just about all forms of SRI. This newer term puts a greater emphasis on the financial goals of the investor.

There's no reason to get caught up in the ever-changing terminology; it's the core principles that are important. However, to expand your overall awareness, here are some other names you may encounter:

- Blended Value
- Ethical Investing
- Impact Investing
- Mission-Related Investing
- Responsible Investing
- Socially Responsible Investing
- Triple Bottom Line
- Environmental, Social, and Governance Screening
- Green or Eco-investing
- Mission-Driven Investing
- Program-Related Investing
- Social Investing
- Sustainable and Responsible Investing
- Values-Based Investing

Here are the definitions for the more popular variations:

Green Investing or Eco-investing prioritizes investing in companies that provide or support environmentally friendly products and practices. These companies encourage (and often profit from) new technologies that support the transition from carbon dependence to more sustainable alternatives while maintaining a commitment to conserving natural resources.

Impact Investing involves financing causes that are of particular importance to investors. Their goals do not necessarily include significant financial gains, and they tend to be more willing than the average investor to settle for below market returns in order to support the advancement of the causes that are meaningful to them.

Socially Responsible Investing has historically been viewed as heavy in religious ideology with a focus on helping investors avoid "sin stocks." While this has been the foundation of the term, a broader and more flexible definition might be more appropriate for investors with different goals. This originally narrow definition is the reason that some have moved towards using the term "Sustainable Investing" or acronyms other than SRI.

Sustainable Investing is a broad term for investment approaches that consider environmental, social, and governance (ESG) factors and their impact, while still prioritizing the rate of return. The ESG criteria allow more than a fundamental fiscal look into a company. They provide additional screens through which we can view the company, giving us insight into its long-term viability. Historically, companies that have higher-than-average ESG scores have outperformed their competitors. In upcoming chapters, I will unpack ESG screens and how to use them.

The definition of SRI found in the courseware of the CSRIC™ designation program is as follows:

> *Any investment strategy that seeks to maximize financial return while simultaneously advancing an idea, belief or cause that is important to the individual investor, with the hope of changing the world for the better (Coombs 2018).*

I like this definition because it aligns perfectly with my personal mission. It directly states that the strategy "seeks to maximize financial return." As an investment advisor, it is clearly important for me to help clients maximize their financial return. Further, this goal is pursued "while simultaneously advancing an idea, belief, or cause." Maximizing your financial return while making an impact is a win-win approach that advisors and clients alike can appreciate. You're able to have your cake and eat it too, by achieving your financial goals while contributing to the betterment of the greater global community.

SRI STRATEGIES

At this point, let's assume that we have answered the question of whether being a socially responsible investor or advisor appeals to you. This leads us to the next question: What is an SRI investor, and what strategies can they employ?

As we discussed, SRI has evolved over the years. The most modern and recent adjustment to SRI is the incorporation of the ESG rating or, as I like to call it, the ESG filter. ESG (Environmental, Social, and Governance) is a screen or filter that can be used in addition to a fundamental analysis, in order to more thoroughly examine a company's risks and opportunities as they relate to the environment and society. I'll expand upon ESG filters in Chapter 5, but you will see some mention of them in the strategies described below.

The following list explains the four major strategies or techniques that investors can use when becoming SRI investors. The ones I will focus on are positive or best-in-class screening, negative screening, and shareholder resolutions. These are strategies that the average person can use to make a significant impact.

Positive or Best-In-Class Screening: This strategy seeks to invest in companies or sectors selected for their positive ESG performance in comparison to their industry peers. This could mean investing in sectors or companies that promote board diversity, sustainable corporate practices, human rights, environmental protections, or local community issues. The difference between this strategy and the negative or exclusionary strategy listed below is that the best-in-class approach will potentially lead to investments in companies that you disapprove of, overall. Those companies are selected because they rank higher or are doing more in specified areas than their peers. For example, if you were seeking to avoid all companies that aren't "green," then a negative screen would create a portfolio without any of the major gas companies. However, in a positive, best-in-class screening, some gas companies may be included if they are ranked best-in-class or have a better ESG ranking than their competitors. This strategy can be used in purchasing mutual funds, exchange-traded funds[iii], stocks, and other equities.

Negative or Exclusionary Screening: In some cases, SRI investors "negatively screen" for businesses involved in areas they wish to avoid, such as alcohol, tobacco, fast food, gambling, pornography, weapons, abortion, fossil fuel production, or the military. Essentially, this strategy will completely exclude certain sectors or companies from the investor's portfolio. This type of screening was the predominant method of SRI for many years.

Community Investing: Community investing is a vital segment of SRI. It seeks to finance projects or institutions that will advance the development of poor and underserved communities in the US and abroad. While this is a fundamentally important topic, it is not an area I will expand upon in this book.

Shareholder Resolutions: Shareholder resolutions are an available strategy for those with shares in publicly traded companies. By filing shareholder resolutions or shareholder engagements and by being involved in dialogue within the corporation, you can greatly influence corporate behavior. As we will explore, when you purchase a minimum number of shares of company stock, you get voting rights at corporate board meetings on topics ranging from environmental issues to electing the next board representative. Groups like As You Sow, Interfaith Center on Corporate Responsibility, and many more organizations help investors pool their votes with like-minded people in order to form a stronger voice, making this approach quite powerful.

The amount of activity and change that has emerged as a result of shareholder activism to date is incredible. This strategy is driving changes within multinational corporations, a feat many assumed to be nearly impossible. These changes range from encouraging major meat producers to invest in alternative meats such as the Beyond Burger, to addressing issues like forced labor, human trafficking, prison privatization, executive compensation, and board diversification. If you own a part of a company, how do you want it to behave? Is it a reflection of you? This strategy and the people using it are encouraging advancements in areas such as racial diversity, gender diversity, water protection, food production, and much more. By investing and becoming an "owner," you have a vote. People all around the globe are using these votes to make real changes.

SUMMARY

Even though SRI may be known by other names, at the end of the day it's still the same concept. Socially responsible investors encourage corporate practices that promote environmental stewardship, diversity, consumer protection, human rights, and animal rights, while anticipating a financial return. It's not a new concept, but the strategies and tools that investors can use have advanced. So, don't get too caught up in the different terms. People like to create new acronyms and cool names for things so they can take credit and seem innovative. I like things simple, so it's SRI in my book, but if you want to create your own trendy name or acronym, go ahead.

FOR INVESTORS: SRI and ESG investing are the wave of the future, both here in the US and abroad. As more and more people realize the power that corporations hold over our environment and political system, they will be arming themselves with the information and tools needed to use their voices to their fullest extent. There are several ways you can make an impact as an investor, so it's important to know what you own and why you own it. I'm going to focus much of this book on ESG screening because the majority of investors are using mutual funds, ETFs (exchange-traded funds), or stock investments. ESG investment options are available and widely used, so I believe this step can have the largest initial impact. Other strategies include shareholder advocacy and proxy voting, which are powerful tools to make your voice heard within the companies you own. Remind yourself that you are an owner of the company, and therefore need to think like an owner about how the company is run and what it needs to improve. Companies have been put on notice that investors are now paying attention, and are equipped with the resources to help drive these corporations in a more sustainable and profitable way. The profit-over-planet mindset is finally dying, and we now have the information and the strategies to put these old ideologies to bed.

FOR ADVISORS: Depending on the clients you work with, the simplest form of SRI involves working with mutual funds, ETFs, or UITs (unit investment trusts[iv]). As an advisor, you should have several good tools available to help you work with clients interested in SRI or ESG investments. The problem in this arena is that there is little standardization among screening and ranking criteria, so you will need to find a system that works for you. I use Yahoo Finance and Morningstar—they have both connected with Sustainalytics to provide ESG and sustainability rankings. Many fund families have ESG/SRI funds on the market, and this is a good starting point as you learn more about options for you and your clients. Not all funds are SRI-equivalent, so you will need to do some homework and compare. There are lots of other resources, many of which we will discuss in upcoming chapters, that will help you work with your clients. In Chapter 6, we'll discuss the US SIF website and the fund screener available there. You can also find a great selection of information and links in the resources section at the back of this book.

4

HISTORY OF SRI

It's impossible to identify when the first act of sustainable or socially responsible investing took place, but I believe it's been happening since the dawn of humanity in one fashion or another. While we don't need to pin down the exact date that SRI began, or what form it took, it is valuable to consider the evolution of SRI and some of the major contributions that have led to what we have today.

Traditionally, SRI has been viewed as investing in organizations that align with your values while avoiding the purchase of stock in companies whose values and activities you don't support. However, socially responsible investing comes in many forms, and these strategies have been used throughout history to promote change. Although I plan to focus much of this book on the investment aspect of SRI, it's important to note there are numerous ways that people have made (and can still make) a sustainable, socially responsible impact merely with their personal choices.

To some extent, all major religions encourage forms of socially responsible investment. Early forms were designed to encourage generosity, compassion, and selflessness, as leaders saw this as a direct reflection of their religious beliefs. One example that I particularly like is from the Jewish holy text, the Talmud, which states that helping a needy person by supporting their business is preferable to giving to charity because investing in another person's livelihood is the highest form of charity. My wife and I live a plant-based lifestyle, and one way we practice this principle is by supporting up-and-coming, sustainable vegan restaurants. These restaurants benefit the local community and the greater environment. By supporting them directly and introducing new customers to their restaurants, we can help stabilize their businesses, which in turn has a positive effect on them and the entire community.

One of the earliest known deliberate large-scale uses of socially responsible investing dates back to the 1758 annual meeting of the Quakers in Philadelphia. Leaders at this particular meeting were addressing their concern over the transatlantic slave trade. They questioned whether the slave trade was ethical, as it was common knowledge that it was very profitable during this time. Ultimately, they decided that the slave trade was not an industry they would support, regardless of the potential for substantial financial gain.

The Quakers subsequently prohibited their members from engaging in any business that would bolster the slave trade. We can see that they were aware that it was a very profitable industry, but they were willing to forgo profit based on their moral compass. There was an extensive, diverse network of abolitionists during that time, engaged in a wide variety of roles, working to end the slave trade. Eccentric abolitionist Benjamin Lay was one, and he laid the groundwork in the decades leading up to this period by actively reminding fellow Quakers that slavery was drastically out of alignment with their values.

This collective decision by the Quakers was an early, powerful example of the potential impact of deliberate investment choices. I believe this one step, by this one group, was an important initial tear in the fabric that had been supporting the slave trade. So, to folks out there with concerns about whether or not you are making a difference, keep moving forward, because our actions today will impact tomorrow.

In the late 1700s, John Wesley gave a sermon called "The Use of Money," which was forward-thinking for the time. He promoted the idea of not doing harm to your neighbor through your business practices, avoiding harmful chemicals that could compromise the health of workers, and avoiding sin stocks that stimulate industries producing guns, liquor, and tobacco. It was considered revolutionary to say, "we ought not to gain money at the expense of life, nor at the expense of our health" (Wesley Center for Applied Theology 1999).

Around 1898, the Quakers followed suit and adopted these practices as well. Many Christian organizations throughout history have adopted or followed some form of socially responsible investing. This focus makes sense when you consider that the Bible contains more than 2,300 verses on money, wealth, and possessions. Jesus spoke about money in roughly 15% of his teachings and in 11 out of the 39 parables. Economics was a popular topic with Jesus.

The trend continued when the Pioneer Fund was introduced in 1928 as the first fund of screened investments. The Pioneer Fund was created by an ecclesiastical group out of Boston and is still active today under the name Pioneer Investments. This fund is an example of the negative screening technique described in the previous chapter. Many organizations now screen for investments that go against their core values. For Christian organizations, this generally means avoiding investments in alcohol, tobacco, and pornography, so they will "screen" their investments to avoid purchasing and consequently bolstering those segments of the market.

During the 1960s, social and political issues helped move SRI into a broader sphere, outside of organized religion. SRI was now being used to address issues such as the civil rights movement, women's rights, and the war in Vietnam. During the Vietnam War, students and protesters put tremendous pressure on universities. They spotlighted their endowments and encouraged them to stop investing in and supporting defense contractors or other companies profiting from the war. Many people from that era remember the famous picture taken in June of 1972 of a naked nine-year-old girl, running towards a photographer, screaming—her back burning from the napalm dropped on her village. This picture led to outrage, not only against Dow Chemical (the manufacturer of napalm) but against a range of companies that were profiting off the war.

By the 1980s, several environmental disasters had caused a growing number to consider the impact of humanity's footprint on the environment. With nuclear incidents like Three Mile Island and Chernobyl, and with pollution on the rise, there was a new level of interest in environmentally friendly investing. These growing concerns had sparked an increased desire to understand how we might reduce our negative impact on the planet.

During this same time, the apartheid system of racial segregation and discrimination was in place in South Africa. Groups such as Calvert Investments, many university endowments, pension funds, various faith-based groups, and others collectively screened and excluded over $620 billion worth of investments to South Africa. This groundswell contributed to the full-scale economic sanctions that were ultimately imposed against South Africa. The resulting negative flow of investments eventually motivated a group of businesses, representing 75% of South African employers, to draft a charter calling for an end to apartheid.

A similar process took place when the US Congress passed the Sudan Accountability and Divestment Act of 2007 to address human rights violations in that region. While the SRI effort alone did not bring an end to apartheid in South Africa, it did help create and focus international pressure on South African businesses. In 1991 apartheid officially ended, and in 1994 Nelson Mandela was elected president of South Africa.

The evolution of SRI has been moving at an unprecedented pace over the last decade. Many countries now consider SRI and ESG-based investing the accepted standard. The UN concluded that "failing to consider long-term investment value drivers—which include environmental, social and governance issues—in investment practices is a failure of fiduciary duty" (PRI 2015). In other words, if you are not using ESG and taking these factors into consideration, you are NOT doing what's in the best interest of the client.

This is an extremely powerful statement, and it sets a standard that the US has not yet caught up to. Consider that carefully. Other countries and the UN feel that advisors who are not using ESG screening criteria may not be acting in the best interest of their clients. So why are so many advisors in the US still failing to use ESG screens and ratings to help their clients? It is gradually catching on here but is heading our way faster than many advisors are prepared for. As we work to catch up, I hope this book motivates readers to talk with their advisors and encourage them to learn more about SRI, so that they can integrate it into their clients' portfolios.

A lot has happened over the course of SRI history, and it all leads us to where we are today. Since 2016, SRI in the US continues to expand at an escalating pace. The total US-domiciled assets under management using SRI strategies grew from $8.72 trillion at the start of 2016 to $12 trillion at the start of 2018, an increase of 38%. This represents 26% or more than one in every four of the $46.6 trillion in total US assets under professional management. I've mentioned this several times already, but want to repeat it to emphasize that this is no passing trend. One in four investment dollars went into SRI-type investments in 2018, and that number is growing. Twenty years ago, I would have doubted this number could be achieved, but now I see it as a sign of a movement that is picking up steam.

Global demand is on the rise for socially responsible investing, and for more education on the topic. This is not a short-lived trend. SRI is still in its infancy, and I envision SRI expanding and improving as more companies and investors discover the value proposition of creating social and environmental change without sacrificing investment return. This growth will accelerate, bolstered by the largest intergenerational wealth transfer in history, now in process from baby boomers to millennials—a population that has reported a strong interest in socially responsible investing. The future is on the doorstep.

SUMMARY

SRI has been around in one form or another since the beginning of time. Its evolution has intensified over the last 30 years, as it has shifted away from the primarily exclusion-based strategy of removing "sin stocks" from portfolios or avoiding direct investment. The methodology has improved through the use of ESG screens, which allow investors to acquire additional information about a company that is not factored into the basic fundamental approach. SRI is growing swiftly in the rest of the world, while here in the US we are catching up, albeit slowly. This comparative sluggishness is largely due to the disproportionate degree of corporate influence allowed by the US government.

FOR INVESTORS: Throughout history, people have been able to "vote" with their dollars. Today, most socially responsible investing involves the use of environmental, social, and governance screens. ESG screens allow you to peel back the layers of the corporate onion to learn more about the companies you are supporting in your portfolio—whether their impact is positive or negative in areas that are important to you. Adding this additional screen is a simple, easy way to give yourself more information on what you own, and how the companies you own are managing their risks.

It seems like a no-brainer that having more information on a company is a good thing. Adding a simple ESG screen is a great first step, and we will learn more about how to do that in the next chapter. SRI has been used throughout history to make an impact and create a legacy, and this is your chance to become part of that story. How do you view the world and what changes would you like to see? What type of legacy do you want to leave?

FOR ADVISORS: I have mentioned it before, but it bears repeating: while over 80% of investors are interested in SRI, fewer than a third of advisors are. That is a big disconnect. In the US as of 2018, one in every four investments dollars was in domiciled assets under management using SRI strategies. So, you can see that this is a positive movement and one that is just picking up steam. I believe that very soon, SRI/ESG investing will be a mainstream practice that will be adopted by many money managers and investors. As you understand how to help clients create SRI portfolios by using the ESG screens, it will become easier to help them move toward a portfolio that aligns with their values. I hope this book provides motivation for you to get involved in this area.

5

WHAT IS ESG? ENVIRONMENTAL, SOCIAL, AND GOVERNANCE

Historically, negative screening—removing or avoiding certain segments of the markets—has been the predominant strategy in the realm of SRI. Essentially, negative screening acts as a shareholder protest to motivate large companies to shift in a healthier direction. In recent years, many money managers and investors have moved away from using purely negative screening while building their portfolios and are now incorporating more environmental, social, and governance (ESG) or best-in-class screens.

Negative screening just pulls out what you don't want, but with the incorporation of ESG screens investors can also find companies that are making positive business moves within the environmental, social, and governance arenas. In my opinion, this is a better system since it places value on companies that are striving to do good versus just removing companies from investment portfolios. In this chapter, we will focus on ESG screening and how it can be utilized by advisors and investors.

Most publicly traded companies are evaluated by how they manage their ESG issues. They are evaluated by third-party providers like Sustainalytics, MSCI, Bloomberg, and others. These publicly traded companies, and now most mutual funds, come with an ESG rating created by one of these outside providers. But what goes into an ESG rating, exactly?

ESG refers to the three central factors used to measure the sustainability and ethical impact of an investment in a company or business. Essentially, ESG provides a set of criteria that investors can use to measure how well a company is managing its risk and opportunities as they relate to environmental, social, and governance issues. That's the definition, but let me make this whole concept very easy to understand. ESG is what I like to refer to as a layer or screen added to already fundamentally analyzed investments. This means that additional information is used in conjunction with the fundamental analysis to view the company or investment from an enhanced perspective.

If you are wondering how all this relates to what we've already learned about socially responsible investing, here is one way to think of the relationship between SRI and ESG: SRI is the mission, and ESG is one available strategy to help you accomplish it. In other words, SRI is a journey to a goal, and ESG is the vehicle you use to travel. So, let's talk a little more about how you can pilot the ESG vehicle successfully to reach your SRI destination.

For example, if I were looking for a stock and found one that looked great fundamentally, had good cash flow, and satisfied all the other measures I was looking for in a solid company, I would then move it into the ESG filter. The ESG filter would allow me to see what other risks or opportunities this company might present that were not visible in the initial fundamental analysis. Just remember, if you start with an already great company with great fundamentals, then you have already developed the groundwork for a good pick. It's a bonus to be able to look at additional data that allows you to view your options from different angles.

So, once I have determined I'm looking at a solid company stock or mutual fund, then I can take it one step further and evaluate it on its ESG criteria. If there are specific areas I want to avoid, such as firearms, pornography, or tobacco, I can also do an additional screen to see how much of the investment is allocated towards those industries. It's that simple. We can take our analysis of a good, fundamentally solid company to the next level of screening by looking at its ESG ratings. Essentially, ESG just supplies additional criteria that investors can use to dig even deeper.

Using an ESG screen allows us to look at how a company manages its risks in relation to environmental and social issues, and this allows us to navigate away from those we feel are poorly positioned for long-term growth. Instead, we can put our focus on finding forward-thinking companies that understand the importance of long-term and consistent growth versus a growth-at-all-costs model. What's more, I'm happy to report that companies with higher ESG standards typically record stronger financial performance and beat their benchmarks, according to research firm Axioma (Aline Reichenberg Gustafsson 2018).

In another example, a study by Bank of America Merrill Lynch concluded that companies with higher overall ESG ratings had lower earnings volatility and higher returns on equity, compared to companies with lower ESG ratings (Bank of America Merrill Lynch 2018). For many, the draw toward socially responsible investing is based on the potential for less risk and an equal or greater return, in addition to the social impact of their investment dollars.

Clearly, companies today are in a tricky situation. Each quarter they are trying to beat Wall Street estimates, which puts many CEOs under the gun to make immediate profits. Because of this, long-term viability is often overshadowed by the dominant growth-at-all-costs mindset. However, the "at-all-costs" model will catch up to these companies and investors eventually, because there is always a consequence to making trade-offs for short-term gain.

To better understand ESG screens and the information they provide, let's talk about what these screens represent and how they can supply us with the additional information to analyze our investments.

ENVIRONMENTAL, SOCIAL, AND GOVERNANCE: DEFINITIONS

E (Environmental) – Climate change, pollution, energy efficiency, deforestation, water scarcity, and depletion of natural resources are some of the areas of focus for investors looking at a company's environmental sustainability. These issues can exemplify risks that are not directly tied to markets. Sometimes these risks are not apparent in fundamental analysis, which is why the ESG filter is an important tool to be used in conjunction with the fundamental analysis.

A significant example of the importance of the environmental screen can be found by looking at the multinational oil and gas company BP. The 2010 BP Deepwater Horizon oil spill was a major and memorable environmental disaster. The Financial Times estimated that cleanup efforts cost the company $90 billion, in addition to the 50% drop in their share price (Financial Times 2013). Investors using ESG screens would likely have avoided this company due to their ESG ratings and the additional information provided.

Looking back, we can see that BP had low performance in safety issues, labor issues, and environmental issues, all information that would have been revealed by employing an ESG filter. Morgan Stanley Capital International (MSCI) excluded BP in 2005 after an explosion in Texas resulted in very little action from BP in the areas of employee safety and environmental safety. This is a prime example of the value ESG can provide, because BP was a thriving company on paper from a fundamental analysis standpoint. Using an ESG screen, however, it could have been anticipated that BP had issues with the potential to backfire catastrophically—which tragically, they eventually did.

S (Social) – This criterion focuses on working conditions, as well as the impact on the community as a whole. Areas of focus include workplace safety, labor relations, workplace benefits, diversity in the workplace, community relations, and human rights.

I like to use a major soft drink company as an example and, to avoid naming names, we will just call them Cola Company. This company's ESG rating is very poor, compared to some of its competitors, due to a combination of controversies over unethical corporate behavior, such as false claims about their products, price fixing, executive misconduct, insider trading, and fraudulent practices. Their impact on communities is ultimately harmful, as they support charities and non-profits on one hand, but lobby against anti-obesity measures on the other. The beverage industry has an extremely strong lobby voice that continues to spread misinformation, denying that their products are unhealthy or that the high sugar content is having a negative impact on society.

The Cola Company serves as a prime example due to the company's wide range of misconduct. But food systems and consumer health, in general, are areas that are particularity important to many millennials. Other areas of concern beginning to come to the forefront of SRI discussions include underpaid workers, exploitation of immigrant workers, human trafficking, gun violence, animal exploitation, gender discrimination, mass incarceration, and the privatization of prisons.

G (Governance) – To gauge the true worth of a company, it's important to explore the effectiveness of its leadership. Areas such as executive compensation, political contributions, and board diversity are also significant. These may all seem like small issues, and many people wonder why they should even care about them. The answer is, all of these factors have an impact on the performance of the company. For example, companies with more female board directors experience higher financial performance, according to the Catalyst Bottom Line Report (Catalyst 2004).

On average, Fortune 500 companies with the highest representation of women in leadership positions attained significantly higher financial performances than those with the lowest representation. Companies with the highest percentage of female board directors outperformed those with the lowest by 53% on their return of equity and 42% on their return of sales. Bottom line, we know that diversity positively impacts a company, and that is why board diversity is one of the leading ESG issues.

Based on corporate filings, Institutional Shareholder Services Inc. (ISS) Analytics calculated that, in the first quarter of 2018 alone, women accounted for 31% of new board directors at the 3,000 largest publicly traded companies (ISS Analytics 2018). The global average of female representation on boards is around 18%. Finland, Iceland, Norway, and Sweden are examples of countries with specific quotas and targets that strengthen gender diversity. Companies operating in those countries face penalties for failing to meet the requirements. This approach has resulted in women occupying around 34% of director positions, almost double the global average (Association for Psychological Science 2016).

Another popular issue that falls under governance is the area of political contributions. Unfortunately, reporting in this area is not mandated by the US Securities and Exchange Commission (SEC), so companies can avoid disclosing information. Many pro-transparency groups are lobbying for this to change, and their efforts have not been in vain. As of 2018, 1.2 million comments have been sent to the SEC asking them to mandate companies to disclose their political and lobbying spending. This is a key issue with wide-ranging effects, and advocates from all across the board continue to push for greater transparency.

An area I choose to focus on is executive compensation. If you own a share of the company and therefore are an owner in the company, wouldn't you want to know what you're paying the person running your company? Wouldn't you want it to be fair and balanced?

The ratio of CEO-to-worker compensation grew to 312-to-1 in 2017, according to a new analysis by EPI Distinguished Fellow Lawrence Mishel and Economic Analyst Jessica Schieder. Average compensation for CEOs of the top 350 publicly traded firms increased 17.6%, while the compensation of the typical worker in these industries rose only 0.3%. My clients find that when they think and act like a partial owner in a company, they care more and pay attention to how the company uses their resources—especially in the form of executive compensation. As a shareholder, you are one of the company's owners, and you have a voice (Economic Policy Institute 2018).

The examples we listed above are just some of the areas that fall under the three main ESG pillars and as the world changes, these areas of emphasis will vary. For example, criminal justice reform, gender justice, and animal rights are just starting to receive the focus they deserve through screening. In one example, FAIRR (Farm Animal Investment Risk and Return) is working to require that companies provide measurements of factory farming by-products and give accurate accounts of negative environmental and social impacts. These factors are taken into consideration in the ESG filters. Data indicates that factory farming is having one of the largest negative impacts on the environment, especially in the area of water usage and pollution. ESG filters are advancing, and further information is being sought after and added all the time.

While ESG ratings are improving, they are still not perfectly comprehensive. One problem with the current ESG filters is that there is no uniformity in how each of the third parties creates their ESG ratings. Each company has its own methodology and, in many cases, this is proprietary information that they resist sharing. Because of this, we currently do not have a uniform methodology that allows us to make standardized evaluations across the board.

In an attempt to make it simple, many groups that provide ESG data report it in a numerical score, although some use an alphabetical grading system (only two groups currently do this). These scores are like the grading systems commonly used in schools, and they can be easier for the average investor to quickly understand and make use of. Unless you are already familiar with the rankings and providers, I recommend you consider starting with Morningstar or Yahoo Finance. Morningstar and Yahoo Finance get their information from Sustainalytics and have created a user-friendly system that is easy to navigate with a little practice. These are valuable tools to apply as you create your SRI portfolio.

We could go on and on about ESG, SRI, and the variety of different strategies, but for most investors and advisors there is only one question they really want answered: does it work? At an ever-growing rate, money managers are incorporating ESG criteria into their investment decisions in order to effectively manage risk. So, you may be wondering, do these professionals know something I don't? The answer is YES.

In fact, there are many sources available that explore the benefits of SRI and ESG screening. Here are just a few examples:

- An analysis of more than 160 academic studies demonstrates that companies with high ratings on ESG factors have a lower cost of capital. Investment managers that have examined and integrated this information into their processes have benefited (Fulton, Kahn and Sharples 2012). The 2012 review by Deutsche Bank Group found that 89% of studies on ESG indicate companies with high ESG ratings show market-based outperformance, while 85% of the studies show accounting-based outperformance.

- Journal of Investing research from 2014 points to advantages of ESG integration in the investment process, finding that active managers can utilize the association between corporate ESG ratings, volatility and risk, and stock return to enhance their stock-picking and portfolio construction ability (De and Clayman 2015).

- Studies suggest that companies with robust ESG practices displayed, over time, a lower cost of capital, lower volatility, and fewer instances of bribery and corruption. Conversely, studies have shown that companies that performed poorly on ESG have had a higher cost of capital and higher volatility due to controversies stemming from incidences including the exploitation of the environment, the exploitation of labor, and various forms of fraud (Nagy, Kassam and Lee 2016).

- Mounting evidence shows that sustainable companies deliver significant positive financial performances. Investors are beginning to recognize and value these companies and their approaches. Arabesque and the University of Oxford reviewed the academic literature on sustainability and corporate performance.

They found that out of the 200 studies analyzed, 90% concluded that good ESG standards lower the cost of capital, 88% show that good ESG practices result in better operational performance, and 80% show that stock price performance positively correlates with good sustainability practices (Fink and Whelan 2016).

- A study of Thomson Reuters ESG dataset by Bank of America Merrill Lynch found that ESG integration can protect investors from bankruptcies, volatility, price declines, and earnings risk. ESG could have helped investors avoid 90% of bankruptcies. Investors that held stocks with above-average ranks on both environmental and social scores would have avoided 15 of the 17 bankruptcies that we have seen between 2008 and 2017 (TruValue Labs 2017).

All of this research drives the point home: ESG-based investing works and is being used by investment professionals all over the world. If you are on the fence and unsure, ask yourself this: if some of the top professionals, fund managers, money managers, and institutional money managers are using ESG to manage their assets, shouldn't I be seriously considering it? If a company is forward-thinking and takes into consideration future liability, they will make adjustments to become more profitable and efficient than similar companies who are not as proactive. It makes sense, right? Time to get off the fence!

ESG factors are fundamentally game-changing for business. Some companies will adapt to this change and succeed, and others will be unwilling to adapt and will fail. The best companies aren't just going to survive; they are going to find a way to thrive. They are innovative and recognize the necessity of a long-term approach, rather than obsessing over short-sighted gains at any cost. They figure out what's going on with water scarcity, climate change, and executive pay and adjust their strategies accordingly. They find ways to reduce risks and cost while discovering smart ways to invest in opportunities for growth with the future in mind. Understanding SRI is not a complex process. It's about finding good fundamental companies that understand the concept of win-win and not just win-at-all-costs.

In 2015 I was able to hear Karina Funk, CFA, give a TED Talk on SRI, and the message she shared was a powerful one. Some of the examples she used are ones I still use when discussing SRI with people today. Here are two of the examples she discussed that encouraged me to find "the win-win." The first involves two truck engine manufacturers, while the second involves a large credit bureau (Funk 2015).

Cummins and Navistar competed in the heavy-duty truck engine market. The companies took opposing views when faced with pollution regulations that required brand new emission control technologies. Navistar believed that the old engine platform was somehow going to meet these new air emission regulations. But they were wrong—and their error came with a high price tag. In 2010, they were fined for every non-compliant engine they were selling. Then it got worse. In 2012 Navistar had to abandon their entire engine platform. To add insult to injury, for every truck Navistar manufactured, they had to begin buying engines from their competitor, Cummins. Navistar became unprofitable and suffered.

Cummins, on the other hand, became a technological leader. They invested early, shortly after the year 2000, in research and development around pollution control technologies. They planned ahead so that they could create engines that were cost-effective and exceeded the new requirements. Because of their technological lead, the stricter the regulations were, the more advantageous it was to them. By being forward-thinking instead of driven solely by a desire for quick profits, they became a leader in their industry. This strategy has helped Cummins surpass the competition on a global scale.

Equifax is an international credit bureau that, at the time of this example, had information on 44% of the US population. When it came to Equifax, ESG groups were issuing warnings about hitches long before hackers gained access to people's personal information. ESG groups were warning people to avoid these shares because the US Consumer Financial Protection Bureau had fined the company for engaging in misleading marketing. They were also weak in governance, specifically in the area of CEO compensation. At that stage, the CEO was paid five times the median compensation for executives in the United States. People who were unaware of these ESG ratings paid the price when their stock tanked. Similarly, Valeant Pharmaceuticals International shares plunged 90% after the company came under investigation for price gouging, among other issues.

As Cummins did in the story above, many other companies have seen the advantage of evolving—like Dow and General Electric. Since 1994, Dow has invested nearly $2 billion in improving resource efficiency and has saved $9.8 billion from reduced energy expenditure and wastewater treatment in manufacturing (McKinsey & Company 2012). By 2013, GE had reduced greenhouse gas emissions by 34% and water use by 47% compared to 2004 and 2006 baselines, respectively, resulting in $300 million in savings (Kline 2014).

Regardless of the company's primary motivation, these changes are beneficial. Whether the individuals running the company actually recognize the importance of being green or sustainable is not as significant as the fact that the company has moved in a sustainable direction. Many companies are still viewing the bottom line through tunnel vision, but they are starting to see the win-win that being socially responsible can bring (Fink and Whelan 2016).

All of these examples serve to demonstrate the impact and opportunity of socially responsible investing. Massive transformation and growth have taken place over the last 20 to 30 years in this discipline. It is being embraced by much of the world and is becoming the standard in many investment communities. While it may be a concept that you're just learning about, or possibly revisiting, you will continue to hear more about it as it grows, evolves, and improves. This is no brief trend. Humanity has begun to recognize that we must care for our shared planetary home.

SUMMARY

Using ESG screens to provide alternative views on investments is a wise decision, as demonstrated by the evidence. ESG investing is a method suited to long-term planning. Some underlying risk factors in your investments may not show their face for many years, while others may be impacting a company right now. ESG screens provide a wider map with which to examine these risks. With shareholder engagement growing rapidly, I believe that more companies will be encouraged to move toward a win-win approach, leaving the win-at-all-costs mentality behind.

FOR INVESTORS: You can use ESG screens from Morningstar or Yahoo Finance to view your current portfolio or to create a new portfolio. Creating a portfolio using ESG screens will help you support companies that show a high ESG score—an indication that they focus on how their business practices impact society and the environment. When you do this, you will be putting less capital in the hands of companies that are focused on quick profits at the expense of the environment and society.

Many people have retirement accounts, and SRI (or lack thereof) impacts most of them on some level. Sadly, few 401Ks or other retirement plans implement SRI strategies. This is an area that is in need of vast improvement. One organization working to improve the situation is Stake. This non-profit group is designing and implementing a platform that will allow investors with mutual funds to impact a company's direction. We will discuss Stake in more detail in a later chapter.

When it comes to retirement plans, many do not offer socially responsible options, and so most people are forced to take the standard route. However, in doing so, they continue to support causes and companies with their investments that they may not support ideologically. The client can push for changes in this area. One route is to talk with your Human Resources Director, or the person in charge of your retirement plan at work, about the inclusion of SRI or ESG screens. A survey from Natixis Investment Managers found that 62% of employees said they would start saving or increase their investments if that also meant doing social good. And, when you look solely at people in the millennial age range (born between 1981 and 1996), the percentage of people who want ESG options is at 84% (Natixis Investment Managers 2016). Here is something to mention in your discussions: implementing ESG options is not only beneficial for the employee, it is also beneficial to the employer since this investment lineup is used to attract and retain talent.

FOR ADVISORS: Clients need information that will empower them to influence their retirement accounts through their employers. It is important to support clients who want to speak with their HR departments about incorporating SRI investments into the fund lineup.

I've found that many employers are very open to the idea, but they are not certain how to go about it. This is where there is an opportunity for the advisor. One great strategy is to find potential investments that may counteract the negative impact a company is having. For example, if the client's employer is a large land developer, you can recommend some SRI funds with a focus on environmental protections in the area of timber, water usage, etc. Clients may recognize that the company they work for does harm in some areas. You can help them become leaders in addressing the damage that has been and is being done, by making changes from within the company. In addition, working with the client and the HR department may allow you access to the general company retirement account, giving you the opportunity to review it to see if there are better options that you can present to your clients.

6

I'M INTERESTED.
NOW WHAT?

My guess is that you haven't been able to put this book down due to its riveting and ever-evolving plot. How could this ever become even *more* exciting? I'm here to tell you it's going to, because we're about to talk about how to pull it all together.

There was a lot to digest in the first five chapters. How do you put all this new information into practice? Before we dive in, I want to repeat the disclaimer: I always recommend you consult a financial planner and, if doing socially responsible or sustainable investing, a CSRIC™ financial planner would be most appropriate due to their specific training in this area. I also recommend consulting with a good tax advisor. Please always consult with an expert prior to making decisions, i.e., implementing anything in this book. I am simply mapping out possible avenues; it is solely up to you to decide which direction is right for you based on your own values, financial objectives, and risk tolerance.

Having issued this caveat several times now, I'm going to proceed under the assumption that you are working with a financial advisor and a tax advisor. I'm also going to assume that by working with a financial advisor, you created a financial plan that outlines your goals, timeline, tax brackets, cash flow, and so forth. By the time you are at this point, you will have a vision of what you need from your investment portfolio, and it's on this solid foundation that you will take your next steps.

Here are the steps you and your advisor should follow as you create your SRI plan:

1. Create a financial plan to determine what your goals are.
2. Determine your risk tolerance.
3. Create your asset allocation^v.
4. Determine the values and issues to support or avoid.
5. Find investments that reflect your values.
6. Regularly review your portfolio to maintain your desired balances.

CREATING A FINANCIAL PLAN

I am a financial planner, so naturally I strongly believe in the importance of planning. Here is a simple analogy: a financial plan is like a road map that shows us the fastest and most efficient route to the destination, or perhaps the direction with the best scenery. Regardless, if you don't have a map you're just driving aimlessly. Yes, you could potentially reach your goal without a map, but it's obviously not the most effective way to do it. A solid financial plan points out the final destination, the potential roadblocks or obstacles you may face, and the possible solutions to those problems. A good financial plan is also flexible, as unforeseen events can happen on any road trip. There are many online tools that can assist you in creating a simple, effective financial plan based on your specific goals.

I believe luck is preparation meeting opportunity.
If you hadn't been prepared when the opportunity came along,
you wouldn't have been lucky.
Oprah Winfrey

I don't describe the planning process in great detail here; the information I present is only meant to act as a starting point. Research indicates that only 19% of workers have considered what they will need to save for a comfortable retirement (EBRI 2018). If you have not calculated what you need in order to retire, please do so. This information is vital and will help you create a safe, comfortable future. It is important to define what you need and then advocate for yourself, but without reliable guidance, planning for retirement can be incredibly challenging. Creating a financial plan can provide you with ideas and direction. For example, it may give you an idea on what rate of return you need to try to achieve to meet your goal. This could help you determine how much risk you should take. This peek into your potential future allows you to anticipate and make adjustments in advance, versus being reactionary.

Planning for retirement requires thinking ahead. But whether you have made time to plan or not, your choice will result in one of 3 possible outcomes:

1. You create a plan, save for retirement properly, and are able to enjoy that time in the future because you prepared for it.

2. You don't plan, and you spend much of your retirement wishing you could go back and do it all differently.

3. You die before retirement, and the people you leave behind either benefit from your planning or have to deal with all your unanticipated loose ends.

If you don't have a plan now, it's essential that you pull your head out of the sand. As a starting point for your financial life and financial decisions, consider creating at least a basic plan. The plan should take into account how many years until you retire, how much money you will need to save, what type of return you will need in order to achieve this, and how long you will be able to live on those funds. You will need to consider what impact inflation and taxes have on your plan, and what happens if death or disability occurs before your projected retirement date. These are just some of the reasons it's important to create a well-thought-out plan.

DETERMINING YOUR RISK TOLERANCE

You will need to determine your risk tolerance in order to have an idea of how to split up the pieces of the portfolio pie, also known as asset allocation. If you're working with a planner, you will complete a risk tolerance questionnaire[vi], and this will let the advisor know how openly or conservatively you want to begin. If you have not taken a risk questionnaire, you can access a risk tolerance test at https://www.calcxml.com/calculators/inv01. There are many tools available to help you calculate your risk tolerance and then create an asset allocation model, but having a trained CSRIC™ advisor is ultimately the best choice.

Investors are human beings and are prone to emotional fluctuations. It's not uncommon for an investor to agree to a portfolio with less risk at a time when they feel more conservative, but after some good returns, they may decide to take more risk. Alternatively, investors agree to a risk tolerance, but after some bad returns, they decide that they really want less risk. Every investment advisor knows exactly what I'm talking about, as investing is as much emotional as it is technical. Whether you're an investment beginner or a veteran, I advise you to determine how much risk you're comfortable with based on your personal situation and stick with it until your risk tolerance or your plan changes. Don't let day-to-day news reports or market swings sway you away from the long-term investment strategy.

CREATING YOUR ASSET ALLOCATION

Once you have determined your individualized risk tolerance, this information is combined with assumptions regarding your tax bracket, timeframe, and goals to produce an asset allocation model personalized to you and your specific circumstances. The asset allocation model will provide the investor with guidance on how much money (i.e., what percentage of your investment) goes into each asset class. This is essentially a way to prevent all your eggs from being in one basket (and thereby exposed to the same risks).

I can't stress the significance of this enough: asset allocation is one of the most important and fundamental aspects of investing. Economists Roger Ibbotson and Paul Kaplan concluded in a 2000 study that more than 90% of a portfolio's long-term returns were driven by its asset allocation. The point being, how a portfolio is diversified can be more important than the actual positions within it.

While I'm not usually a fan of rules of thumb, there is one frequently given for asset allocation. The rule is this: take your age and subtract it from 110 in order to find out what percentage of your money should be in equities. The remainder should be in fixed income, with some cash for those at or approaching retirement. For example, if you're 40 years old, the rule suggests that 70% of your portfolio should be invested in equities (110 - 40 = 70), with the other 30% in fixed income. To be clear, this is a general idea and not a substitute for more precise asset allocation tools. The problem with the result of the rule-of-thumb calculation is that it is too general. You have the suggestion that you should invest 70% of your portfolio in equities, but now you must answer the questions: What equities? International or domestic? Large-cap or small-cap? Growth or value? This is where a good allocation tool or a good advisor is truly necessary. So, let's continue beyond the rule of thumb, and focus on an example of a hypothetical client who took a risk-tolerance questionnaire and has determined their risk tolerance.

We'll use the example of a fictitious Mr. X. Mr. X took a risk-tolerance quiz online that said he was a "moderate investor." Let's pretend, based on his risk tolerance, that he would be most comfortable splitting up his assets in the following manner: 65% equities, 35% fixed income, and 0% cash. You can see the pie chart representing his results, below. If you did your own risk tolerance analysis, your resulting graph would likely look different from this example.

Recommended Allocation

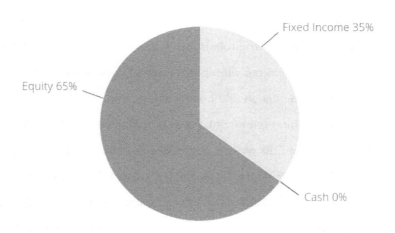

Figure 1. This pie chart shows the recommended allocation model for our hypothetical Mr. X.

This is a traditional style pie chart, which shows the potential diversification or asset allocation for our sample investor. The pie chart used in this example is a simplistic version—other pie charts you find may include more details.

Let's talk about diversification[vii]. Diversification means splitting your money amongst different asset classes. Many people think it's just about having money in different baskets, however, true diversification is about using different investments within the different asset classes. For example, if you have $100 and you buy four different stocks, all of them in technology, you may feel that you have diversified. But, while you may have four different stocks, they are all within the same sector. If the technology sector struggles, then you would suffer in all of your baskets. Even though you bought stock in four different technology companies, you're still not very diversified. If you invested in both equities and bonds, your equities (in this example, your technology stock) could struggle, but that need not impact your entire portfolio. Ideally, you want to find investments with some form of inverse relation to each other, meaning that your investments are not directly mirroring each other, in order to balance your risk.

So, true diversification means varying things within your asset classes. But what does that mean? What are the options available to you within each class? To help you understand this, let's discuss each asset class and what it might contain. The following list contains the three main asset classes—equities, fixed income, and cash—and some subcategories you are likely to encounter while creating a portfolio:

EQUITIES (STOCKS): I like to say that if you are investing in equities, you are "an owner, not a loaner." Equities represent shares of ownership in businesses, and they're typically the most volatile of the three types of assets (although the range of risk varies greatly within this category).

Historically, equities have outperformed other asset classes over long periods. This makes them good investments for money you won't need to access in the near future. Here are some of the different types of equities available:

VALUE STOCKS

Companies perceived to trade at a discount to their peers. They're generally considered to be well-established businesses with strong fundamentals.

GROWTH STOCKS

Companies that are growing faster than average and therefore offer the potential for greater returns than value stocks, as well as a greater risk of losses.

LARGE-CAP STOCKS

Generally speaking, companies whose market capitalization is $5 billion or greater, though some definitions set the threshold higher or lower.

MID-CAP STOCKS

Companies with market caps of $1 billion to $5 billion.

SMALL-CAP STOCKS[VIII]

Companies with market caps of less than $1 billion.

INTERNATIONAL STOCK FUNDS[IX]

Funds that invest in companies based outside the US.

GLOBAL STOCK FUNDS

Funds that invest in companies globally, including in the US.

EMERGING-MARKET FUNDS[X]

Funds that invest in stocks based in rapidly growing, young economies. Countries like China, Brazil, and India are examples of emerging markets, as opposed to developed economies like the US, the UK, and France.

FIXED INCOME (BONDS): If you are invested in bonds or fixed income, you are "a loaner, not an owner." Fixed-income assets make regular interest payments based on an agreed-upon interest rate. These payments may stay the same (fixed rate) or may change over time (variable rate), depending on the type of asset. For example, inflation-protected bonds make higher payments when inflation occurs. Generally speaking, fixed income assets are less volatile than stocks, but this does not mean they are risk-free.

As with equities, there are several different types of fixed income investments:

GOVERNMENT BONDS

Bonds issued by the federal government, such as treasury bonds.

MUNICIPAL BONDS

Bonds issued by local governments.

CORPORATE BONDS

Bonds issued by corporations to fund their operations. Depending on the company's credit rating, these can be extremely stable, extremely risky, or anywhere in between. High-quality bonds are known as investment grade.

SHORT-TERM BONDS

Bonds that mature within five years. All other things being equal, longer maturities typically translate to higher interest rates, but increased volatility.

INTERMEDIATE-TERM BONDS

Bonds that mature in five to ten years.

LONG-TERM BONDS

Bonds that mature in ten years or more.

CASH: This category refers to physical cash, as well as interest-bearing vehicles such as savings and money market accounts. Even if cash investments bear interest, their returns generally don't keep up with the rate of inflation, making them poor long-term investment vehicles. Cash investments are typically appropriate for money that is needed soon, or money that you absolutely cannot afford to lose. I usually only recommend cash investments for people who are in or near retirement and even then, only as a small percentage of their portfolios (Frankel 2017).

If you are working with an advisor, they will diversify amongst the three major asset classes, and will probably also take your asset allocation down to the subcategories level. If you are doing this on your own, you should consider doing so as well.

MR. X EXAMPLE

So, now that we understand what is involved in the various asset classes let's go back to our friend, Mr. X. Remember, this is a fictitious example. Do not base your own allocation on this hypothetical scenario. After taking his risk tolerance questionnaire, Mr. X receives an allocation model based on his risk tolerance, timeframe, tax bracket, and goals, which shows him how to consider splitting up the pie. In this example, Mr. X is told that he should consider the following allocation:

FIXED INCOME	**35%**
Domestic Fixed Income	20%
International Fixed Income	15%
EQUITIES	**65%**
Large Cap	30%
Small/Mid Cap	15%
International	20%

The allocation model suggests that Mr. X put 65% of his money in equities (specifically large cap, mid and small cap, and some international), and keep 35% in fixed income or bonds.

Mr. X now has an idea of how much money he should invest in different areas of the market. He has a solid idea of how much risk he is willing to take. So, the next step is for Mr. X to find the right funds or stocks to fit those allocations. He can move forward with confidence, now that the space and structure have been created for him to choose investments based on his values.

DETERMINING THE VALUES AND ISSUES TO SUPPORT OR AVOID

This is where the process becomes highly personalized and when talking to an advisor about your goals can be especially beneficial. To start the actual construction of an SRI portfolio, we want to determine the values and screens that you want applied to your portfolio. This can easily be done with a questionnaire, or just by knowing your own areas of interest and concern. There are no right or wrong answers because you are designing a portfolio to support what you care about, not to fit into someone else's way of thinking. This is where you move away from investing purely for profit and into the realm of investing for purpose *and* profit. You're growing it for your future, so what impact do you want to make with it?

When working with my clients, I like to start the process with a questionnaire to establish a list of their values and interests. What do they have a passion for? What do they want to avoid? Everyone is different, and this set of questions allows us to get specific and typically leads to additional constructive dialogue. These conversations are fantastic opportunities for me to truly understand my clients and what they are trying to accomplish. Working with passionate people who want to make an impact is what motivates me to do what I do.

There are many organizations that can help you screen for values and issues, using over a hundred different categories. For example, you may have an issue with an investment in weapons, but perhaps that is too broad. Do you have an issue with handguns, semi-automatic rifles, bump stocks, chemical, or biological weapons? For each major category, there can be several subcategories. The available screening may not be perfect but, whatever your faith or politics, you should be able to find screens that work for you.

You'll find a sample questionnaire on the next page. As you can see, it allows you to select from a variety of environmental, social, and governance issues. This will help you and your advisor to have a conversation about your interests and find investments that reflect your goals and values.

SAMPLE INVESTOR VALUES QUESTIONNAIRE

Place a check mark next to any issues that you would like to consider in your investments:

COMMUNITY

- [ ] Affordable Housing
- [ ] Community Relations/Philanthropy
- [ ] Community Services
- [ ] Fair Consumer Lending
- [ ] Microenterprise
- [ ] Small and Medium Businesses

SOCIAL

- [ ] EEO/Diversity
- [ ] Health and Safety
- [ ] Human Rights
- [ ] Labor Relations
- [ ] Forced and Child Labor
- [ ] Terrorist or Repressive Regimes
- [ ] Indigenous Peoples' Rights
- [ ] Other

GOVERNANCE

- [ ] Board Issues
- [ ] Executive Pay
- [ ] Political Contributions
- [ ] Bribery and Corruption
- [ ] Other

ENVIRONMENT

- [ ] Renewable Energy and Alternative Energy Technologies
- [ ] Climate Change/Carbon
- [ ] Green Building/Smart Growth
- [ ] Pollution/Toxics
- [ ] Natural Resource and Water Conservation
- [ ] Other

PRODUCTS

- [ ] Alcohol
- [ ] Animal Testing/Welfare
- [ ] Faith-Based
- [ ] Weapons and Firearms
- [ ] Gambling
- [ ] Nuclear
- [ ] Pornography
- [ ] Product Safety
- [ ] Tobacco
- [ ] Other

The questionnaire gives you an opportunity to consider the specific areas you want to support and areas you want to avoid. It may also show you areas that you have not previously considered. With any plan or vision, it's important to take the time to reflect and write it down. This is a great starting point for you and your advisor to discuss in more depth what type of impact you want to make in each of these areas, and what your options are.

FINDING INVESTMENTS THAT REFLECT YOUR VALUES

Nothing is flawless, so your portfolio could represent your core values but might still contain companies that you have issues with. It's difficult to find the "perfect" fund that invests in everything that you want and avoids everything that you don't. This is common because we are all unique and have unique interests. Speaking as someone who is passionate about animal welfare, ideally I want to find funds that avoid investments in factory farming or other industries that harm animals. Unfortunately, animal welfare screens are rarely used, but I am hopeful that this will change as more people become aware of the immense environmental damage caused by large-scale animal agriculture. Perhaps you are passionate about clean energy and are looking for funds or investments that avoid some of the major polluters, but that also seek out companies with positive carbon ratings. Christians might screen or search for funds that avoid alcohol or that embrace and support ministry work, and so forth.

Animal rights is one example of an area where finding a mutual fund that supports my specific values would be hard. The only way around this is by creating a stock portfolio where you can select each stock individually, based on how they match up to your values. If you have an interest in animal welfare, consider the site crueltyfreeinvesting.org, which lists the majority of publicly traded companies and screens them for animal welfare issues. They also have created a list of advisors or companies that have created "vegan" or animal-cruelty-free portfolios. I have a portfolio on that site and felt it was important to provide this option since there are very few screens or funds currently available for animal welfare.

So, animal welfare is something that I'm passionate about. Whatever you are passionate about, you may also find that the fund options could be limited in that specific area. In that case, working with an advisor to create a potential stock portfolio could be especially valuable to you. If you work with an expert, they may use stocks, mutual funds, bonds, or a combination of many investment vehicles. This book focuses on keeping it simple when starting this process, and so it makes sense to work with mutual funds or ETFs[xi] that are already screened. There are enough SRI funds out there now to meet most people's financial needs *and* represent their values.

Before we get into specifics, it's once more time for the caveat. As mentioned, I am legally prohibited from giving you specific investment suggestions in this book. I do not know anything about your particular situation. My goal is solely to provide research tools and examples that increase your understanding of the process. If you're an advisor, these research tools can help you expand your use of SRI with clients who want to match their values to their investments.

What follows are some effective, simple ideas on how to take your list of "wants and avoids" and find suitable investments that meet your criteria. If you are working with a CSRIC™ advisor, they may have some additional strategies not mentioned here. What I present below are some of the main options, which are great starting points and can be as effective as other, more complicated strategies.

USING AN SRI/ESG MUTUAL FUND PORTFOLIO

With the list of preferences and restrictions you've selected, one option is to utilize sustainable or socially responsible mutual funds or exchange-traded funds. A mutual fund is a fund that gives small or individual investors access to professionally managed portfolios of equities, bonds, and other securities. The average mutual fund holds hundreds of different securities, which means mutual fund shareholders gain important diversification. Each shareholder participates proportionally in the gains or losses of the fund. Mutual funds pool money from the investing public and use that money to buy other securities, usually stocks and bonds.

Socially responsible or sustainable mutual funds are like any other mutual funds, except that they screen companies against or for areas related to environmental, social, and governance issues. There are many groups out there that create and manage SRI/ESG portfolios that are aligned with the values of their clients and that also match their risk tolerance and asset allocation.

One helpful method for selecting a fund is to use a mutual fund screening tool. For instance, US SIF provides a Mutual Fund and ETF Performance Chart that displays all sustainable, responsible, and impact mutual funds and ETFs offered by their institutional member firms. This publicly available tool allows individual investors to compare cost, financial performance, screens, and voting records of competing funds. It won't list every single fund, but it's a solid list. All funds listed are open to new investors.

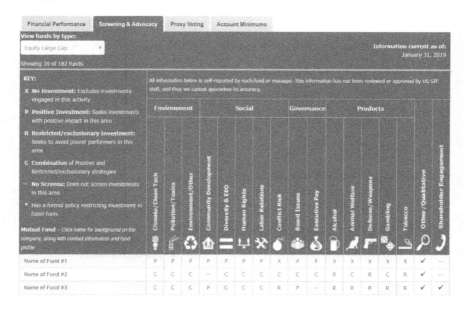

Figure 2. This screenshot shows the basic layout of the ESG screening tool available on the US SIF website (US SIF and Bloomberg 2018).

Figure 2 shows the ESG screening tool on the US SIF site, which contains 182 funds in the large-cap category. There are many funds to choose from, and you can navigate this tool with minimum effort. The chart is laid out based on the SRI strategies we discussed earlier, such as negative screening or positive investments. Listed in their respective categories are issues of ESG, such as climate, pollution, human rights, conflict risk, animal welfare, gambling, tobacco, etc. The sections below each category reveal how (or if) fund managers address each issue in their portfolios. This tool is powerful because it provides information about the manager's ESG and investment strategies, and also notes their performance, cost, and other important information. Of course, past performance does not necessarily indicate or reflect future results.

If you are working with an advisor, it's important that they understand that not all SRI funds are the same. They do not all work uniformly or all screen in the same ways. Calling the company directly is another way that the investor or advisor can learn more about the screening process of a particular fund. Each mutual fund creates a document that states the direction of the fund, what it's screening, what it's including, etc., and you can get much of this information over the phone. Don't feel reluctant to call the company and ask questions about their methodology of screening and selecting investments. Some thoughtfulness and patience at this stage will pay off in the long run.

Another simple strategy to consider is the use of an asset allocation fund or a target date ESG/SRI fund. These funds are what I refer to as "funds of funds" because they usually appear to be just one fund, but they actually contain several other mutual funds/investments. In essence, it's diversified based on specific timeframes or risk tolerances. For example, you will see some funds listed as blends, such as Blend 60% S&P500[xii]–40% BC Aggregate. This means that the fund is 60% equities and 40% bonds. If that meets the investor's risk tolerance, the investor might want to simplify and use this asset allocation fund to reach the goal. With a little research and digging, you may be able to find some asset allocation funds that fit your personal allocation goals. As more and more groups start creating SRI/ESG funds, we will see many more of these timeframe or risk-based strategies emerging.

Mutual funds are a great way to begin since most investors are already somewhat familiar with them. They are the predominant investment in most people's workplace retirement accounts, such as 401Ks, 403Bs, or IRAs. However, unlike the standard fund that is solely designed to make a profit for the investor, the SRI/ESG portfolio is designed to make a profit *and* make a constructive social impact.

Unfortunately, most workplace retirement plans do not offer SRI or ESG-based options. This is something we would like to see change and adding your voice can help bring that about. Most groups have access to SRI/ESG funds, but they just need to be encouraged to make the call and have them included in their list of options. If you are willing to be proactive and speak up, you may be able to bring about this change in your own workplace.

Finally, there are several other tools you might consider when creating an SRI portfolio. I use Morningstar, which now shows sustainability ratings on funds and stocks, as well as Yahoo Finance. Sometimes the best information comes directly from the source, so consider calling the fund company directly, or working with an advisor who is in contact with a number of these fund managers and who understands the fund's objectives, goals, and screens.

USING STOCKS OR INDIVIDUAL EQUITIES

Another option is to create an SRI portfolio using individual stocks or securities. I usually recommend people consider starting with ESG funds or UITs because they are simpler for the beginner. However, if this is an area you or your advisor is already comfortable with, there are some simple strategies for working with individual stocks and equities that you can consider. One way to approach this is by digging into any of the ESG or SRI mutual funds to find their holdings. You will find that many mutual funds and UITs will show their stock positions. Investors can make use of this information, recognizing that the fund companies have likely already done their research. You may find that by looking at several similar funds, you will start to see patterns. For instance, each of your large-cap funds may contain many of the same stocks.

So, some investors choose to list out the mutual funds that fit their screens and then search for recurring stocks or patterns, looking to see if the fund managers in different funds are buying the same stock. For example, if you are looking for a solid large-cap stock choice, you might look at several large-cap mutual funds and see if there are stocks they all have in common. Of course, finding a stock this way doesn't guarantee that it's a great stock, but it does make it more likely. You will know that these fund companies put it in the portfolio for a reason, likely because they feel it has potential. It's not uncommon for investors or advisors to create an entire portfolio using this process.

Beginning with mutual funds and ETFs is a good way to go if you'd like to keep the process simple. If you decide to use individual stocks instead or in addition, consider creating a well-diversified mix of equities. For my portfolios, I generally use at least 20–30 stocks or equities, depending on the overall portfolio size. Ultimately, it is your responsibility to do your research and decide how to proceed. After all, it's your money, and no one else is going to engage with it to the extent you do.

From a compliance and ethical perspective, I cannot give you specific advice about fund choices. Therefore, I cannot provide examples of a completed mutual fund portfolio or a completed stock portfolio. With the information I've provided, you should be on your way to creating your own SRI portfolio. With a few clicks, you could easily conduct an internet search for ESG, UITs, ESG mutual funds, etc. and you will find information on what's out there in the market. Online, you can determine the composition of some professional portfolios, and you can use them as examples. As always, I recommend working with a professional. This book is an educational tool that can be helpful or lead to trouble if used incorrectly.

PROFESSIONAL COMPENSATION: COMMISSION-BASED, FEE-ONLY, FEE-BASED

If you are working with a professional, it's important to understand how they are compensated. Are they commission-based, fee-only, or fee-based? These are terms you may hear financial advisors use to describe how they are compensated for their work.

Commission-based advisors or brokers earn commissions for recommending certain mutual funds, annuities, or other investment products. The commission rate could be anywhere from 2 to 7%, depending on the product. In some instances, this comes right off the top of the investor's investments. In other cases, this could be paid to the broker or advisor directly from the company whose product they sold or recommended.

Fee-only advisors or RIAs (registered investment advisors) don't sell products or investments, therefore they do not receive commissions. Fee-only advisors may be paid a percentage of the assets they manage, a fixed fee paid either annually like a retainer fee, or hourly. Fees for managing clients' assets could range anywhere between .05% to 2% or more, depending on the client, the case, the amount of assets, and so forth.

Fee-based advisors are a blend of the previous two categories. Like a commission-based advisor, they can sell investment products for which they might receive a commission when they deem it appropriate. And like the fee-only advisor, they can charge a fee based on the percentage of assets they manage.

Not all advisors are compensated the same way, so it's important to have this discussion with your advisor. This knowledge may help you understand not only how (or how much) you will be charged for their services, but also why they may be using certain products or providing certain advice. Of course, it makes sense to consider finding an advisor with expertise or a designation in the area you are interested in, such as a CSRIC™ designation from the College for Financial Planning. If you are driven by SRI values, then advisors with SRI-specific designations like this are more likely to have knowledge and interests that align with your goals.

SUMMARY

There are many ways to go about creating a sustainable or socially responsible investment portfolio. This chapter was intended to give you a foundation to continue learning. There are many tools out there that folks can access to help them in this journey. I want to point out that much of this chapter, although dedicated to SRI, is based on fundamental financial planning and investment concepts.

It makes sense to create a game plan first and then determine the direction of investments. A financial plan will lay out your financial data and hopefully will also uncover your value drivers, which give your portfolio a starting point and direction.

Other fundamental investment concepts we discussed include asset allocation, risk tolerance, and the basics of how mutual funds work. While this is just a taste, hopefully it will entice you to dig further. The resources listed at the end of this book can help.

FOR INVESTORS: I use the analogy that even though I know how to change the oil in my car, it's not something I want to do. It's an important job, and to me personally, it is worth it to compensate someone else to take care of that job. You may feel the same way about financial planning and investment planning. While you may have the skills to create and monitor your own SRI portfolio, do you want to? Recognizing choice is empowering. You have the choice of trying this on your own or collaborating with a financial professional. The terms and concepts in this book can spark central talking points for you to discuss with your financial advisor.

FOR ADVISORS: You are already familiar with many of the concepts I described in this chapter, such as asset allocation, financial planning, risk tolerance, and so forth. Some areas you may not be as familiar with, such as how ESG screens work and how to utilize them to help a client meet their investing objectives and align their investments with their values. There are some great free resources out there, including US SIF, Morningstar, and Yahoo Finance, and a quick search will reveal many more.

If much of this is unfamiliar to you, no problem. We are all new at something. A great place to start is US SIF. They have an inexpensive course you can take that will give you an additional framework to amplify your base knowledge. As I mentioned, ESG is just an additional layer used to screen an already fundamentally solid company. So, if you have the fundamentals of investing, then learning some ESG basics will not be too difficult. Understanding the ever-changing landscape is another story but, as with anything else, you will get much better with practice and time.

The connection to a community of people who are striving to make an impact is one of the greatest benefits of this type of investing. I love all my clients, but the clients who have a passion for socially responsible investing are particularly exciting to work with, and they can really bring out our own personal passions for change as advisors. I hope this chapter has succeeded in outlining a simple path you can take to evolve your work with your clients and contribute to productive global change.

7

SHAREHOLDER ADVOCACY

I have been working as an advisor in the financial industry for over twenty years. During that time, I've had very few discussions with peers about shareholder advocacy. It is not a popular topic of conversation yet. Many advisors are unaware of how shareholder advocacy operates, the strength of the process, and the significant impact it has behind the scenes. And honestly, I was not aware of the full extent of its impact either, until I had a really powerful conversation with someone immersed in this aspect of sustainable investing.

After becoming familiar with shareholder advocacy, I now consider it to be one of the most powerful vehicles available for large-scale change. In this chapter, I will describe how shareholders and organizations are using their stock shares to drive change in business practices. This strategy can create pivotal change on the corporate level by empowering individual shareholders to work together. In a world seemingly ruled by corporate giants, many people feel that as individuals, they have no say and no impact. But shareholder advocacy and dialogue are powerful, effective tools that the so-called "small fries" can use to amplify their voices. Shareholder activism is a critical strategy available for making positive change, but it is currently underutilized. The best way to address this is by educating investors about their rights, as this book aims to do. As a shareholder, your existing rights provide you with a variety of tactics to engage a corporation with your vision for progress. These actions can range from direct dialogue with the company to large-scale letter-writing campaigns—but the tactics we will focus on in this chapter are shareholder resolutions and proxy voting.

PROXY VOTING

When you purchase shares in a publicly traded company, you become a part-owner of that company. With that status comes certain rights that you can use to address environmental, social, and corporate governance issues within the company. Each year, at the company's annual general meeting (AGM), resolutions are put up for a vote. Prior to the AGM, companies issue a proxy statement (sent directly to investors by mail or email) with the agenda and the detailed information regarding what will be voted on. Shareholders have the option to vote in person; however, most investors don't travel to the annual board meetings. Instead, they have an opportunity to vote through proxy voting. Voting by proxy allows investors to cast their votes without being physically present in a process similar to casting an absentee ballot.

When you fill out your proxy as a shareholder, you specify how you would like your vote to be cast on the company's proposals or resolutions. Resolutions put forward by the company typically focus on electing directors, executive compensation, and other routine items. In contrast, shareholder resolutions are more focused on ESG-related issues such as political spending practices, human rights, climate justice, etc. Often, shareholders can also vote on proposed changes to the operation of the company, such as shifting corporate goals or other structural changes. Shareholders have the right to vote on matters that directly affect their stock ownership, such as a company's proposal for a stock split, merger, or acquisition.

Investors can vote on resolutions that impact areas they feel strongly about. Some common focal areas are gender diversity on the board of directors, executive compensation, political contributions, and overall environmental standards. Increasingly shareholders realize that ideology aside, these are issues that can impact their stock value and their returns. So, whether their motivation is the future of the planet, or just the bottom line, being a part of the discussion is often in their best interest.

When you exercise your right to vote and impact the company's direction, you are taking part in the process referred to as "shareholder advocacy." If you do not vote for or against resolutions as an investor, you are not influencing management, and they can continue to do business as usual. By exercising your rights as a shareholder, you can communicate with management, policymakers, and board members. This process is a direct way to influence companies to consider changes or to hold them accountable to their course if the path is already a healthy one.

Through shareholder advocacy, awareness increases and advancements take shape. Massive improvement doesn't happen overnight, and there is no instant gratification. Behind every large societal shift, there is a multitude of small steps and individual conversations that create ripple effects in the world.

With an understanding of the process and the possibilities, this area of socially responsible investing is where you can make one of the largest impacts on how companies do business. I hope that this chapter will inspire you to make use of the available tools and allies so that you, the average investor, can use your power to create change. When one person holding a few shares in a company is combined with thousands of like-minded shareholders, they form a voting force that cannot be ignored.

In the past, shareholders rarely took advantage of their right to proxy voting, and when they did, it was often just to blindly cast their votes in favor of the company's board recommendations. Fortunately, this has been changing; as more investors participate in strategic proxy voting, they are beginning to dramatically impact corporations and how they do business. The more individual shareholders and money managers that participate in this practice, the more powerful this tool will become.

One flaw in this current system is that many investors, while they may own shares of companies, own them through a mutual fund or other investments—not solely as a company stock. Many of the investments the average person has in retirement accounts are through their employer, such as in a 401K. Unfortunately, if you own a stock through a mutual fund, then you automatically give up your voting rights to the fund manager. This means that you may own a share of a company through your mutual fund, but this is not the same as owning individual stocks, and you don't have the same rights.

Many money managers or advisory groups have policies dictating that they automatically vote with the management of the company. So, if their fund contains shares of Company X, the money managers will vote however the management of Company X recommends. This practice is founded in the belief that management knows best and will always do what is in the company's best interest. But management's view of what is best can often be short-sighted; most of the time, company management will vote against the advancement of social and environmental issues, as they don't feel they are relevant. So, if you own stock through a mutual fund, you are handing over your voting rights to the fund manager. And chances are, unless it's an ESG fund, the fund manager is not voting based on your values or concerns.

With the majority of assets in the hands of money managers, it can be difficult to get the votes needed to pressure management to bring about change. There is no shortage of serious environmental, social, and governance issues that corporations need to address, and the urgency is only increasing. Despite the growing pressure, research shows that in 2015, nine of the 42 leading mutual funds failed to support a single shareholder proposal on climate change (Coombs 2018).

The good news is that in 2018, many of these groups began to step up in the area of environmental and climate issues. Large investment firms are beginning to address gender diversity on boards, climate justice, and other ESG factors. They have put corporate leaders on notice that ill-informed business-as-usual practices will no longer be acceptable.

These recent policy shifts may be significant and refreshing; however, they are still not enough. Large-scale funds are at the center of many people's retirement plans. With many shareholders either abstaining from voting or simply voting with management, a huge opportunity is being wasted. Without the engagement of the greater population, a small number of people will continue to control the votes, the policies, and billions of dollars.

Recently, I learned about an organization called Stake that takes a fantastic and unique approach to shareholder advocacy. Stake began as a student-led organization and was founded by Gabe Rissman—the first student to file a shareholder resolution—and his Yale classmate, Patrick Reed. They shared a passion for environmental advocacy and began by campaigning for their university to improve its investment policies. Eventually, Gabe and Patrick joined forces with Cary Krosinsky, a professor of sustainable investing. Krosinsky helped them to write an academic paper on creating the most impact through investing, and ultimately became the third co-founder of Stake.

Stake is taking shareholder advocacy to a new level by attracting financial advisors and their clients that own mutual funds, and they are leveraging those mutual fund shares to encourage the mutual fund companies to support sustainable investing. Their work could be instrumental in moving large fund companies in the direction of sustainability. This change in direction would, in turn, lead to more accountability for the companies in the mutual fund portfolios. This is exciting news since many of the votes are in the hands of these fund managers. Imagine the leaps forward in SRI and impact investing if the largest fund companies were all supporting sustainability in their investments.

Until Stake gets the rest of the large fund companies on board, there are already some mutual funds and ETFs that utilize ESG screens, and also provide proxy voting to shareholders based on a set of published criteria. These organizations will map out their proxy voting guidelines and their voting history. This information is available to you, and it is extremely helpful in determining if a fund you are interested in is voting on issues that you believe are relevant. If you are interested in exploring such funds, one great resource is the US SIF Mutual Fund website. They break down many socially responsible mutual funds and will outline exactly what issues they are voting on, and their mandates for voting. Different funds will have different agendas and goals. For myself, I always look into how the fund manager deals with animal welfare, the treatment of animals in the entertainment industry, and factory farming. Some funds will factor in and vote on these issues, and others will not.

You may wonder, if I only own a little bit of this company, why would they listen to me? While it may seem far-fetched for the average investor to impact a company, it happens all the time. When you combine one person who holds a few shares in a company with thousands of like-minded shareholders, you have created a solid and audible voting force. However, many people remain uninformed about the specifics of proxy voting. For those of you who still have questions, I've listed the answers to some of the more common ones, below.

PROXY VOTING F.A.Q.

Q: Can I assign my vote to someone else?

A: Yes—in most cases, as a shareholder, you can assign your voting rights to a third party and still maintain ownership of the shares. If you do so, you allow the third party to vote for you.

Q: Why would someone assign their vote to someone else?

A: One reason shareholders may want to delegate their vote is to assign it to someone who is more informed and prepared to speak on the subject that is being voted on. Another possibility is that shareholders want to take advantage of the option of pooling their votes with others for greater impact—an option which we will discuss in more detail below.

Q: If I own a stock, how do I pool my votes together with other investors?

A: There are many organizations, such as Interfaith Center on Corporate Responsibility (ICCR); As You Sow; Glass, Lewis & Co; Institutional Shareholder Services (ISS); and others, that help institutional and individual investors maximize their proxy votes. These groups allow shareholders to delegate voting authority to a representative who can vote on their behalf. This strategy, known as pooling votes, allows these groups to have more influence with public corporations. These organizations are at the forefront of shareholder advocacy, although their work is still underappreciated and unknown to many, even within the financial planning community.

Q: I just own a couple of shares in a company. Can I really make an impact?

A: The organizations mentioned above bring together shareholders like yourself to create a large voting bloc. They use this combined voting power to effectively influence issues of importance, or specific resolutions they may be proposing to a company. These organizations have more sway and a louder voice than the individual shareholders would when acting independently. So, regardless of the number of shares you own, you could be a part of a significant, powerful group that is a force for change.

Q: How do I know which issues these organizations are working towards, or what resolutions they are proposing?

A: Each of these organizations provides a list of all the resolutions they support and a report outlining where they stand on the issues. The data presented on each organization's website can be filtered based on the particular issues you want to address. For example, if you want to know which organizations are addressing the use of antibiotics in the meat industry, you can use a filter to see which companies they have resolutions with and how they are engaging with those companies on that specific issue. If you own shares in one or more of those companies, a shareholder advocacy organization can help you to use those shares to encourage changes in that area.

Q: Is it really worth assigning or pooling your votes? Is real change happening?

A: The answer to these questions is an emphatic YES! There is ample evidence of real change, brought about by advocacy groups using the pooled voting strategy. As You Sow, founded in 1992, is the nation's non-profit leader in shareholder advocacy. They have racked up an impressive tally of successes, all made possible by a collection of committed individuals, large and small investors alike. As You Sow's advocacy has seen successful change in significant organizations such as Exxon, Palmolive, Procter & Gamble, and Disney, to name just a few. You'll find a list detailing some of their most impressive wins a little later in this chapter.

SHAREHOLDER RESOLUTIONS

As was mentioned at the beginning of the chapter, another strategy for shareholder advocacy is using shareholder resolutions. Shareholder resolutions can be filed after dialogue with the company has failed, and it's time to take the next step. The issue can be framed as a resolution and, if approved by the SEC, will then be voted on at the company's AGM. Once the votes are counted, there are several possible outcomes. If the resolution receives less than 3% of the vote, then it will be dismissed, and you will not be allowed to bring it back to the board for another three years. If it receives more than 3%, then it can be voted on again at the next year's AGM. If there are enough votes for the resolution to pass, each company has specific by-laws that describe how to proceed. However, in many cases winning the majority vote is not necessary in order to help direct change. Many company directors will recognize the support for an issue once a resolution is proposed and will make adjustments accordingly.

I want to pause here for a moment to reflect on the power of this approach. In some cases, resolutions don't even need to come to a vote. Sometimes just the act of filing can bring attention to an issue, and this can lead to conversations and potential agreements with management. If the filer of the resolution feels the issue is going to be addressed or taken seriously, they may withdraw the resolution.

For example, the Interfaith Center on Corporate Responsibility (ICCR) stated in its 2018 Resolutions and Proxy Voting Guide that they had over 266 member-sponsored resolutions that year (ICCR 2018). Of those 266 resolutions, ICCR had 61 successful withdrawals, with the potential for more. This type of result confirms that companies see the power of shareholder advocacy. Companies are beginning to work with advocacy groups to address issues in advance, avoiding a more public discussion. Some of the top issues that are being addressed today are climate change, alternative energy, diversity, political contributions, and lobbying. Other recent resolutions have focused on gun safety measures, paid family leave, and prisoners' rights.

There are other organizations also working proactively to enable shareholders to direct their impact to areas that matter to them. Corporate Accountability is an organization that connects people globally to address systemic inequality and economic injustice by strengthening democracy and holding transnational corporations accountable. They state, "We are building a world rooted in justice where corporations answer to people, not the other way around—a world where every person has access to clean water, healthy food, a safe place to live, and the opportunity to reach their full human potential" (Corporate Accountability 2018). Worth Rises is also creating social change and providing tools for shareholder advocacy. Their report titled *The Prison Industrial Complex: Mapping Private Sector Players* currently identifies over 3,900 corporations profiting from America's prison system (Worth Rises 2019).

In many cases, corporations welcome shareholder advocacy because they see the benefit of adjusting to this more thoughtful and collaborative approach. In some instances, they now recognize the benefit of changes they may have initially objected to. In other cases, they just make agreements to avoid bad press. Those in charge of corporations are increasingly demonstrating a willingness to reach out to organizations to learn what they can do to foster healthier business practices and to improve their ESG rating. As more investors adopt SRI or ESG-based strategies, corporations will be increasingly motivated to enter into constructive dialogue, as the benefit of engaging with this large segment of investors becomes clear.

As You Sow

Shareholder advocacy groups like ICCR and As You Sow are on the front lines, campaigning for change. These groups have made major strides in showing how powerful shareholder advocacy can be. The following is a sampling of As You Sow's many successes—it is not a complete list (As You Sow 2018). These victories are game-changing and impact every one of us:

- 2011: McDonald's agrees not to use nanomaterial in their food.
- 2013: McDonald's agrees to end the use of foam beverage cups at all 14,000 US locations.
- 2013: Whole Foods announces it will label all GMO foods in stores by 2018.
- 2013: Keurig agrees to make all K-cups recyclable by 2020.
- 2014: Exxon agrees to publish the first-ever report on its exposure to carbon asset risk, sparking more than 400 media stories

and launching the concept of "carbon asset risk" in the global consciousness.

- 2014: Palmolive agrees to make all packaging recyclable in three of four divisions by 2020.

- 2014: Procter & Gamble agrees to make 90% of its packaging recyclable by 2020.

- 2015: Disney agrees to stop showing images of smoking in films targeted toward youth.

- 2015: Southern Company, one of the country's largest utilities, commits $2 billion in renewable energy development.

- 2016: Resolutions were filed with Wells Fargo, Goldman Sachs, and Morgan Stanley, to stop financing companies participating in the Dakota Access Pipeline and to increase protection of the rights of Indigenous Peoples.

- 2016: Chipotle announces a 50% food and packaging waste diversion goal by 2020.

- 2017: KFC, Burger King, and Wendy's sign agreements with As You Sow, agreeing to purchase only chicken raised without superfluous antibiotics.

- 2018: Dunkin' Donuts agrees to phase out foam cups by 2020, removing nearly 1 billion foam cups from the waste stream every year.

- 2018: Brinker agrees to phase out the use of antibiotics in their chicken.

- 2019: Sanderson Farms agrees to phase out antibiotic use in their chicken.

I have great respect for As You Sow. This organization has been lifting up the shareholder voice to increase corporate responsibility on a broad range of environmental and social issues for decades. Their mission is summed up in the statement: "We harness shareholder power to create lasting change that benefits people, planet, and profit" (As You Sow 2018). This statement boldly illustrates the opportunity and impact that shareholder advocacy can have.

I was fortunate enough to have the opportunity to speak recently with the president of As You Sow, Danielle Fugere. The phone conversation I had with Danielle was eye-opening and humbling for me, as I realized that I still had so much to learn about the crucial role played by organizations like As You Sow. While Danielle and I were talking, some breaking news came in. She was notified by Sanderson Farms that, after many years of dialogue and advocacy, they would end the use of antibiotics in their chicken. Even though Sanderson Farms did not officially acknowledge the validity of the scientific research presented, they did agree to end their use of antibiotics. To have organizations like Sanderson Farms and other major chicken producers agree to end antibiotic use is a major victory and a giant step forward in the battle for cleaner food. Danielle told me that their work is not finished at this point. They will continue to work toward cleaner pork and beef and to end the use of unnecessary antibiotics.

Danielle brought up another interesting issue during our conversation, the issue of nanomaterial in food. I had never heard of the consumer issues surrounding this practice. This is an example of an invisible yet important issue that affects our health. As You Sow commissioned an independent study in 2013 that tested ten types of powdered doughnuts and found a nanoparticle called titanium dioxide in Dunkin' Donuts powdered cake doughnuts. Dunkin' Donuts is now in the process of removing the nanomaterial after coming under pressure from As You Sow, whose efforts included putting a proposal before parent company Dunkin' Brands' shareholders (Strom 2013).

You, the shareholder, are a crucial part of these steps forward. This is real, fundamental change. Transformation doesn't come about through pointless complaining; change is the result of thoughtful reflection and constructive actions leading to sustainable core changes, which have an actual impact on your life and millions of other lives. For me, realizing the true strength of shareholder advocacy was stunning. I already had a passion for the topic, but my appreciation for these organizations that are fighting for direct change has been taken to a new level.

Shareholder advocacy

When I've discussed shareholder advocacy with peers, some have expressed concern. They believe shareholder engagement could hinder the overall success of companies they are investing in. Here, it is important to question your definition of "success." Is it rapidly plowing forward with only a profit motive? Or, is it mindfully taking steps to ensure a healthier world? When I asked Danielle about the criticisms, she commented that shareholders are largely engaging with these companies with rational conversations. She also noted that companies often request that advocacy groups inform them in advance about what issues will be brought up. This way, companies are able to take the time to prepare to address them. It's promising news that some companies want to know this information. They may start off just wanting to avoid liability, but might come to start genuinely caring about the issues being raised. Shareholders have the choice to make their voices heard, and when they do, real change can happen.

Remember, if you own stocks through one of the traditional mutual funds, either on its own or through your workplace retirement plan, that vote is going to be dictated by the money manager running that particular fund. So, it's important to find out who the fund manager is for any funds you are invested in, and what they are voting on, if in fact they are voting at all. You might also consider learning more about groups such as Stake, who can use your mutual fund shares to motivate the fund companies to use or consider more ESG measures.

If you own stock and are not receiving a proxy ballot, speak with your advisor, because they may be receiving the proxy ballots for you. Make sure you relay your interests to your advisor. Then, you can align your values with your stocks and your votes. You and your advisor can work together to create a systematic process to utilize those votes the way you, the shareholder, wish to.

I hope you see the power in being a shareholder, and thereby part-owner of a company. With power comes responsibility, and that responsibility applies whenever we have a vote. I believe I have the responsibility as a citizen to do my due diligence and research political candidates so that I can make an educated vote at election time. It is no different for a stock owner with shareholder rights—you should educate yourself on the issues in order to cast your vote responsibly. Many groups covered in this book share information on upcoming proxy votes, what companies are having which kind of votes, and when. More and more information is now available to the average investor. The opportunity for change through advocacy has never been as powerful.

Many groups use shareholder advocacy to promote change by purchasing shares in companies that they may not support but want to influence. One of my favorite examples of this is Green Century's collaboration with other organizations and individual investors to influence Tyson Foods to invest in alternative meat options. As a result, Tyson became a major shareholder in Beyond Meat, one of the most popular meat alternatives. This decision has the potential to have a tremendously positive impact further down the road because the demand for meat alternatives is on the rise. In many cases, executives or boards are simply unaware of consumer interests and concerns. By adding a meat alternative to their lineup, Tyson has increased its diversity and therefore decreased its risk. All meat producers will face the growing pressure on factory farms and industrialized farming as their detrimental environmental effects become common knowledge. Shareholder advocacy is set to play a major role in this large-scale change.

SUMMARY

When you pool voices and votes with millions of others, you can make an impact in ways many people can't imagine. It's happening every day behind the scenes, while most investors remain unaware. Shareholder engagement, corporate resolutions, and petitions are incredible tools that are making change possible on the major social justice issues of our time.

FOR INVESTORS: If you own shares, then you have potential votes. If you want to vote within a particular company, you can purchase shares in that company to give yourself the right to vote. If you have causes you want to support or issues you want to address, you can use organizations like the ones mentioned in this chapter to find out what companies they are monitoring and working with to generate change. You can even work with many of these organizations to have them vote on your behalf. The bottom line is that real change is happening, and it's happening because of everyday people. Shareholders are awakening; investors are no longer staying silent and ignoring the frequent, ignorant actions taking place in the corporate world.

FOR ADVISORS: You have an opportunity to make a meaningful impact in the lives of your clients on many levels. You can choose to motivate and encourage investors to pay attention to what they own. As you engage clients in conversations on a multitude of topics, you will learn about their interests, passions, and concerns. Helping clients invest in a way that brings their passions to the table builds a meaningful, trust-centered relationship between advisor and client. Selfishly, many advisors are not doing this. If you are passionate about truly helping people to invest in alignment with their values and utilize shareholder advocacy, that is wonderful. Unfortunately, with that vision, you will find that you are currently in the minority of advisors. I recommend that you do some research on groups like As You Sow, Stake, and the others mentioned above. You may find an area of financial planning and wealth management that provides the opportunity for impact, which could very much resonate with your current client base, if only they knew what's possible. I'm convinced that once a client creates a plan, implements the plan, aligns their investments with their values, engages with the companies, and begins using their shares to create change, these clients are likely with you for the long term. This approach sets you apart from the average advisor who lacks understanding of SRI issues and options.

8

THE FUTURE OF SRI

Before we talk about the future, let's first take a small step back in time. In 2015, leaders from 193 countries came together at the UN Headquarters in New York to discuss the future of the planet and how we, as a global community, can face some of the most daunting challenges. They acknowledged that war, disease, famine, drought, and poverty are issues that have a global impact and affect everyone's communities.

The leaders at this gathering knew that billions of people were being impacted by systems that could be changed for the better. They affirmed that, while natural disasters are inevitable, this does not mean that high death tolls are acceptable. They acknowledged that there is enough food to feed the world, yet much of the world does not have access to enough food. And, while there are medications to fight diseases, many people cannot afford the medicines they need.

These leaders believed that by working together, we could create a brighter future, and they believed that billions of people around the world shared their vision. At the conclusion of this meeting, the group produced the 2030 Agenda for Sustainable Development, a platform that listed a total of 17 Sustainable Development Goals (SDGs) to be achieved by 2030. The goals are ambitious but vital, and the progress they have made continues to give me hope. The United Nations Development Program (UNDP) is one of the organizations leading the charge to meet the SDGs by the 2030 deadline.

Figure 3. This infographic from the United Nations shows the 17 global goals included in the 2030 Agenda for Sustainable Development (United Nations 2015).

The future of SRI looks bright with so many nations supporting these world-saving plans. The Principles for Responsible Investment (PRI), developed with the assistance of the United Nations, was launched in 2006 at the New York Stock Exchange, and initially included only 100 signatories. As of 2019, that number has climbed to more than 2,300 signatories, which include asset owners and investment managers from around the globe. The first of the six PRI principles is: "We will incorporate ESG issues into investment analysis and decision-making processes." The number of PRI signatories, the global support for the 2030 Agenda for Sustainable Development, and the overall direction of the UN on these issues are all indicators of a paradigm shift towards compassion. It shows a desire to transcend dualistic thinking and move past the us-versus-them mentality.

When I began writing this book in 2016, the reported total for ESG investments in the US was estimated at around $8.7 trillion, which was one in every five investment dollars at the time. Now, as I finish this book at the beginning of 2019, the US SIF has recently released its 2018 Report on US Sustainable, Responsible, and Impact Investing Trends. Investors now consider environmental, social, and governance factors across $12 trillion of professionally managed assets, a 38% increase since 2016, and the reported sustainable and impact investing in the United States continues to grow.

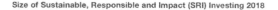

US|SIF   Sustainable and Impact Investing —
                Overview

Size of Sustainable, Responsible and Impact (SRI) Investing 2018

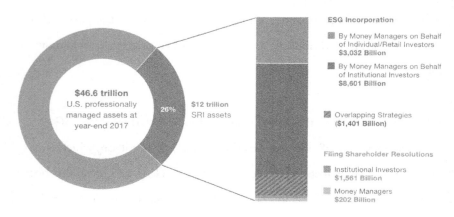

Figure 4. This chart shows the breakdown of assets in the SRI segment (US SIF Foundation 2018).

Since 2016, asset managers and investors have increasingly addressed a growing number of social and environmental issues. According to a recent survey from the Morgan Stanley Institute for Sustainable Investing and Bloomberg, a majority of US asset managers are now practicing sustainable investing and view it as a strategic business imperative. Specifically, 75% of respondents revealed that their firms had adopted sustainable investing, compared to 65% in 2016 (Morgan Stanley Institute for Sustainable Investing & Bloomberg LP 2019).

Matthew Slovik, Head of Global Sustainable Finance at Morgan Stanley, said in a press release that "The survey results demonstrate that sustainable investment strategies are now a strategic imperative," and

"It is clear that asset managers will continue to invest new resources and expand their product portfolios in the coming years" (Bloomberg LP 2019).

The notion that managers now view SRI as a "strategic business imperative" is a powerful one. This means that this is no short-term trend; rather, money managers are now taking the stance that SRI is in demand, and the demand is only increasing. Gun violence, gender discrimination, environmental harm, and other issues will be increasingly addressed through the various SRI processes that we have explored throughout this book. Unfortunately, while large-scale asset managers are becoming more aware and active, the majority of independent advisors are not yet on board. Nevertheless, this major shift confirms that interest in ESG-based investing is taking root here in the United States, and it points to a promising future.

As individual investors become more aware of SRI opportunities, financial companies recognize that they must create products to fit the need. This drives financial advisors and other professionals to keep up with the movement and to become well-versed in SRI. As technology improves, the investment opportunities improve, and companies become more engaged in the practice of socially responsible investing.

The chart below shows how SRI and ESG-based investing has taken off over the last decade.

FIGURE A

Sustainable and Responsible Investing in the United States 1995–2018

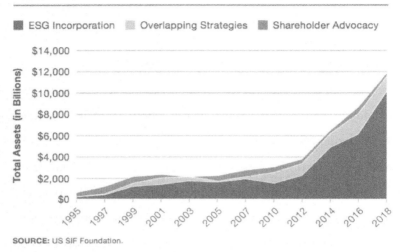

SOURCE: US SIF Foundation.

Figure 5. This graph produced by US SIF shows the growth of SRI within the US since 1995, with a sharp increase in growth beginning in 2012 (US SIF Foundation 2018).

As you can see in the chart, gradual growth was replaced by much more rapid progress around 2012, with no signs of slowing since. As always, the economy will ebb and flow, but the data suggests a bright outlook for SRI. I believe that one day, ESG screens and SRI will simply be considered "investing" and we won't need the additional qualifiers. Once taking care of the earth finally becomes the norm, we will arrive at that place where all investing is an investment in the best interests of people and the planet as a whole.

In case you think that this is just one person's wishful thinking—I'm not the only one making this prediction. In November 2018, BlackRock CEO Larry Fink suggested that all investors would be using ESG metrics within five years (Feloni 2018). That's a bold prediction, but it is not far-fetched. What's more, BlackRock, along with Vanguard, didn't stop there. Both groups, as well as several other large money managers, have made strong and direct public assertions about what they expect from companies in the ESG realms of board diversity, climate change, and other areas. These groups bring a lot of power to the fight, considering that BlackRock and Vanguard hold stock in nearly every publicly traded company.

Factory farming and animal welfare

I'd like to add a small section for my plant-based and vegan friends, or anyone interested in animal welfare. In my opinion, animal welfare—and specifically factory farming with its associated environmental damage—is sorely under-represented within the current ESG filters. Very few fund companies incorporate screening for animal welfare, which is surprising given the overwhelming scientific evidence showing the negative impact large factory farming has on the environment. Sadly, many fund managers point to a lack of demand as the reason so few groups screen for this. This lack of attention to animal welfare has led me and some of my peers to design our own ESG portfolios that take animal welfare into consideration. Organizations such as The Humane Society, PETA, and Cruelty Free Investing also provide information on companies and their treatment of animals.

Only a small percentage of the US population is vegetarian or vegan. Due in part to ag-gag legislation, many investors are unaware of how their food is produced and the environmental impact of the current meat-production methods. Ag-gag laws make it possible for businesses to sue farmers who speak out to expose abuses inflicted on their farms. These laws are a major obstacle preventing farmers and others from being able to implement healthier farming methods. Currently, factory farming dominates the meat industry and has an enormously detrimental effect on the environment. The general lack of coverage in the media and the existing ag-gag laws ensure that the public remains largely unaware of the practices and problematic outcomes of factory farming. As with the many other issues we've discussed, investors can be the drivers of change in this area.

The number of Americans who identified as vegan increased from 1% to 6% between 2014 and 2017, an increase of 600% over three years. These figures are from a report, *Top Trends in Prepared Foods 2017*, by research firm Global Data. The report noted that the increased vegan population and rising awareness of the negative impact of meat consumption were driving demand for meat-free products and meat substitutes. They suggested that as people connect ethical, sustainable lifestyles with good health and overall wellness, the demand for ethical production throughout the food chain will continue to grow (Global Data 2017). As with many of the issues we've discussed, it will take people working together to create the pressure to move companies and mutual funds away from these industries. Awareness is increasing; I believe that as more consumers see the environmental impact of factory farming, this issue will reach a critical mass and the large-scale change will begin.

Animal welfare is an issue that is personal to me. Yours may be based on values of your faith, environmental factors, diversity, political transparency, or a combination of many issues. Whatever your focus, you can use the same tools to make an impact, and I hope that this book has provided you with both the means and the motivation to start along that path. Of course, SRI is not yet everything that it could be. The movement is still in its early stages, and there is currently no set standard for ESG reporting. But while SRI and ESG screening are not perfect, they are constantly growing, improving, and evolving, and at a speed that many financial advisors in the US are unprepared for. If you are one of those individuals—investor or advisor—who were previously unaware of the speed and direction of this extensive SRI movement, then I hope this book has left you feeling more informed.

I have found that being involved in socially responsible investing has brought me closer to my clients. Learning from my clients has been, and continues to be, a fascinating and valuable experience that has broadened my awareness of local and global challenges. This growth has impacted my life, the lives of my clients, and many others. Work becomes joyful when it is in support of the greater good, so it is my hope that this book will encourage at least a few other advisors to look at investing differently. Enthusiasm for new revelations might motivate advisors to present SRI strategies to their clients, who might then go on to create their own impact. Investor or advisor, you have a part to play. The question is, where do you fit in the future of SRI? Remember, the change starts with you.

ENDNOTES

i Neither Asset Allocation nor Diversification guarantee a profit or protect against a loss in a declining market. They are methods used to help manage investment risk.

ii Mutual Funds are sold by prospectus. Please consider the investment objectives, risks, charges, and expenses carefully before investing in Mutual Funds. The prospectus, which contains this and other information about the investment company, can be obtained directly from the Fund Company or your financial professional. Be sure to read the prospectus carefully before deciding whether to invest.

iii Exchange Traded Funds (ETF's) are sold by prospectus. Please consider the investment objectives, risks, charges, and expenses carefully before investing. The prospectus, which contains this and other information about the investment company, can be obtained from the Fund Company or your financial professional. Be sure to read the prospectus carefully before deciding whether to invest.

iv Unit Investment Trusts (UIT's) are sold by prospectus. Please consider the investment objectives, risks, charges, and expenses carefully before investing. The prospectus, which contains this and other information about the investment company, can be obtained from your financial professional. Be sure to read the prospectus carefully before deciding whether to invest.

v Asset Allocation does not guarantee a profit or protect against a loss in a declining market. It is a method used to help manage investment risk.

vi Risk tolerance is an investor's general ability to withstand risk inherent in investing. The risk tolerance questionnaire is designed to determine your risk tolerance and is judged based on three factors: time horizon, long-term goals and expectations, and short-term risk attitudes. The adviser uses their own experience and subjective evaluation of your answers to help determine your risk tolerance.

vii Diversification does not guarantee a profit or protect against a loss in a declining market. It is a method used to help manage investment risk.

viii Smaller capitalization securities involve greater issuer risk than larger capitalization securities, and the markets for such securities may be more volatile and less liquid. Specifically, small capitalization companies may be subject to more volatile market movements than securities of larger, more established companies, both because the securities typically are graded in lower volume and because the issuers typically are more subject to changes in earnings and prospects.

ix Investing internationally carries additional risks such as differences in financial reporting, currency exchange risk, as well as economic and political risk unique to the specific country. This may result in greater share price volatility. Shares, when sold, may be worth more or less than their original cost.

x Investments in emerging markets may be more volatile and less liquid than investing in developed markets and may involve exposure to economic structures that are generally less diverse and mature and to political systems which have less stability than those of more developed countries.

xi Mutual Funds and Exchange Traded Funds (ETF's) are sold by prospectus. Please consider the investment objectives, risks, charges, and expenses carefully before investing. The prospectus, which contains this and other information about the investment company, can be obtained from the Fund Company or your financial professional. Be sure to read the prospectus carefully before deciding whether to invest.

xii Indices are unmanaged and investors cannot invest directly in an index.
The Standard & Poor's 500 (S&P 500) is an unmanaged group of securities considered to be representative of the stock market in general. It is a market value weighted index with each stock's weight in the index proportionate to its market value.

GLOSSARY

2030 Agenda for Sustainable Development – In 2015, the UN Assembly produced 17 goals and 169 targets to wipe out poverty, fight inequality, and tackle climate change by the year 2030

401K – A retirement savings plan, with contributions deducted from the employee's paycheck

403B – A retirement savings plan available for employees in certain sectors, including public education, non-profit, cooperative hospital service organizations, and self-employed ministers

Ag-Gag Laws – Laws that currently exist in seven states, penalizing whistleblowers who investigate the day-to-day activities of industrial farms

AGM – Annual General Meeting: an annual meeting held by a corporation, open to all of its shareholders, where resolutions will be voted on

Asset Allocation Fund – Funds with mix of assets appropriate for specific risk tolerances

CSRIC™ – Chartered SRI Counselor™ designation, from the College for Financial Planning

ESG – Environmental, Social, and Governance

ETF – Exchange Traded Fund: an investment fund that is traded on stock exchanges, much like stocks, but may contain a mix of assets such as stocks, commodities, or bonds

FAIRR – Farm Animal Investment Risk and Return

IRA – Retirement account at a financial institution with tax-free growth or on a tax-deferred basis

ISS – Institutional Shareholder Services Inc.

PRI – Principles for Responsible Investment

RIA – Registered Investment Advisor

SDGs – Sustainable Development Goals, part of the 2030 Agenda for Sustainable Development

SRI – Socially Responsible Investing

Target Date Fund – A fund that seeks to grow assets over a specific period

UIT – Unit Investment Trust: an exchange-traded mutual fund offering a fixed portfolio of securities having a definite life

UNDP – The United Nations Development Program

US SEC – US Securities and Exchange Commission

RESOURCES

As You Sow - https://www.asyousow.org

College for Financial Planning - https://www.cffp.edu

Corporate Accountability - https://www.corporateaccountability.org

Cruelty-Free Investing - http://www.crueltyfreeinvesting.org

Glass, Lewis & Co. - https://www.glasslewis.com

The Green Money Journal - https://www.greenmoneyjournal.com

The Humane Society - https://www.humanesociety.org

Institutional Shareholder Services Inc. - https://www.issgovernance.com

ICCR (Interfaith Center on Corporate Responsibility) - https://www.iccr.org

Jennifer N. Coombs CRPC™ - https://www.gradmoney.org

Karina Funk, TEDxWilmington Talk - https://youtu.be/fno1QluA6EQ

Kate Raworth, Doughnut Economics - https://www.kateraworth.com

KMF Advisors - http://www.kmfadvisors.com

Morningstar - https://www.morningstar.com

PETA (People for the Ethical Treatment of Animals) - https://www.peta.org

Risk Tolerance Calculator - https://www.calcxml.com/calculators/inv01

Stake - https://www.yourstake.org

Sustainalytics - https://www.sustainalytics.com

UN Sustainable Development Goals - https://sustainabledevelopment.un.org

US SIF (The Forum for Sustainable and Responsible Investment) Mutual Fund and ETF Chart- https://charts.ussif.org/mfpc

Worth Rises - https://worthrises.org

Yahoo Finance - https://finance.yahoo.com

BIBLIOGRAPHY

Aline Reichenberg Gustafsson, CFA. 2018. *Companies with strong ESG scores outperforms, study finds (Financial Times)*. August 12. Accessed 2018. https://nordsip.com/2018/08/12/companies-with-strong-esg-scores-outperform-study-finds-financial-times/.

As You Sow. 2018. "About Us." *As You Sow*. Accessed 2018. https://www.asyousow.org/about-us.

Association for Psychological Science. 2016. *Putting Corporate Quotas to Work for Women*. July 19. Accessed 2018. https://www.psychologicalscience.org/news/minds-business/putting-corporate-quotas-to-work-for-women.html.

Bank of America Merrill Lynch. 2018. "Environmental, Social & Governance (ESG) The ABCs of ESG." August 10. Accessed 2018. https://www.bofaml.com/content/dam/boamlimages/documents/articles/ID18_0970/abcs_of_esg.pdf.

Bloomberg LP. 2019. "Sustainable Investing Goes Mainstream: Morgan Stanley and Bloomberg Survey Finds Sustainable Investing A Business Imperative Among U.S. Asset Managers." *Bloomberg LP*. February 21. Accessed 2019. https://www.bloomberg.com/company/announcements/sustainable-investing-goes-mainstream-morgan-stanley-bloomberg-survey-finds-sustainable-investing-business-imperative-among-u-s-asset-managers/.

Catalyst. 2004. "Report: The Bottom Line: Connecting Corporate Performance and Gender Diversity." *Catalyst, Workplaces that Work for Women*. January 15. Accessed 2018. https://www.catalyst.org/research/the-bottom-line-connecting-corporate-performance-and-gender-diversity/.

Coombs, Jennifer N. 2018. "Module 1: Shareholder Advocacy." In *CSRIC Accreditation Textbook*, by College for Financial Planning, 11.

Corporate Accountability. 2018. *Corporate Accountability: Who We Are*. Accessed 2018. https://www.corporateaccountability.org/who-we-are/

.
De, Indrani, and Michelle Clayman. 2015. "The Benefits of Socially Responsible Investing: An Active Manager's Perspective." *The Journal of Investing* 24 (4): 49-72.

EBRI. 2018. "2018 Retirement Confidence Survey." *Employee Benefit Research Institute*. April 24. Accessed 2018. https://www.ebri.org/docs/default-source/rcs/1_2018rcs_report_v5mgachecked.pdf?sfvrsn=e2e9302f_2.

Economic Policy Institute. 2018. *Top CEOs' compensation increased 17.6 percent in 2017*. August 16. Accessed 2018. https://www.epi.org/press/top-ceos-compensation-increased-17-6-percent-in-2017.

Feloni, Richard. 2018. "BlackRock CEO Larry Fink says within the next 5 years all investors will measure a company's impact on society, government, and the environment to determine its worth." *Business Insider*. November 1. Accessed 2018. https://www.businessinsider.com/blackrock-larry-fink-investors-esg-metrics-2018-11.

Financial Times. 2013. *Claims may push BP's spill bill to $90bn.* February 5. Accessed 2018. https://www.ft.com/content/097ca8f4-6f6b-11e2-b906-00144feab49a.

Fink, Carly, and Tensie Whelan. 2016. "The Comprehensive Business Case for Sustainability." *Harvard Business Review.* 10 21. Accessed 2018. https://hbr.org /2016/10/the-comprehensive-business-case-for-sustainability.

Frankel, Matthew. 2017. "Here's How to Determine Your Ideal Asset Allocation Strategy." *The Motley Fool, LLC.* May 28. Accessed 2018. https://www.fool.com/ retirement/2017/05/28/heres-how-to-determine-your-ideal-asset-allocation.aspx.

Fulton, Mark, Bruce Kahn, and Camilla Sharples. 2012. "Sustainable Investing: Establishing Long-Term Value and Performance." *SSRN.* June 12. Accessed 2018. https://ssrn.com/abstract=2222740.

Funk, Karina. 2015. "Sustainable Investing: What you didn't know could make you money. [Video File]." *TEDxWilmington.* October 28. https://www.youtube.com/watch?v=fno1QIuA6EQ.

Global Data. 2017. "Top Trends in Prepared Foods 2017: Exploring trends in meat, fish and seafood; pasta, noodles and rice; prepared meals; savory deli food; soup; and meat substitutes." *CISION PR Newswire.* June 22. Accessed 2018. https://www.prnewswire.com/news-releases/top-trends-in-prepared-foods-2017-exploring-trends-in-meat-fish-and-seafood-pasta-noodles-and-rice-prepared-meals-savory-deli-food-soup-and-meat-substitutes-300478350.html.

ICCR. 2018. "ICCR's 2018 Proxy Resolutions and Voting Guide." *Interfaith Center on Corporate Responsibility.* 01. Accessed 2018. https://www.iccr.org/iccrs-2018-proxy-resolutions-and-voting-guide.

ISS Analytics. 2018. "Female CEOs on a Glass Cliff? A Look at Gender Diversity and Company Performance." *ISS Analytics.* October 26. Accessed 2018. https://www.issgovernance.com/library/female-ceos-on-a-glass-cliff/.

Kline, Daniel B. 2014. "Green Technology is Paying Off for GE." *The Motley Fool.* March 5. Accessed 2018. https://www.fool.com/investing/general/2014/03/05/ green-technology-is-paying-off-for-ge.aspx.

McKinsey & Company. 2012. "The Business of Sustainability." *McKinsey & Company.* Summer. Accessed 2018. https://www.mckinsey.com/business-functions sustainability/our-insights/the-business-of-sustainability-mckinsey-global-survey-results.

Medland, Dina. 2017. "Europe Accounts For Over Half Of $22.89T Global SRI Assets As Sustainable Investing Takes Off." *Forbes.* March 27. Accessed 2019. https://www.forbes.com/sites/dinamedland/2017/03/27/europe-accounts-for-over-half-of-22-89-tn-global-sri-assets-as-sustainable-investing-takes-off.

Morgan Stanley Institute for Sustainable Investing & Bloomberg LP. 2019. "Sustainable Signals: Growth and Opportunity in Asset Management,." *Morgan Stanley.* February 19. Accessed 2019. https://www.morganstanley.com/auth/content/dam/ msdotcom/en/assets/pdfs/2415532-Sustainable_Signals_Asset_Mgmt-FINAL.pdf.

Nagy, Zoltán, Altaf Kassam, and Linda-Eling Lee. 2016. "Can ESG Add Alpha? An Analysis of ESG Tilt and Momentum Strategies." *Journal of Investing* 25 (2): 113-124.

Natixis Investment Managers. 2016. "Running on Empty: Attitudes, Actions, and Assessments of Defined Contribution." *Natixis Investment Managers.* November 21. Accessed 2018. https://www.im.natixis.com/us/resources/2016-survey-of-defined-contribution-plan-participants.

Nuveen. 2018. "Fourth Annual Responsible Investing Survey." *Nuveen, A TIAA Company.* October. Accessed 2019. https://www.nuveen.com/fourth-annual-responsible-investing-survey.

PRI. 2015. "Fiduciary Duty in the 21st Century." *Principles for Responsible Investment.* September 8. Accessed 2018. https://www.unpri.org/fiduciary-duty/fiduciary-duty-in-the-21st-century/244.article.

Strom, Stefanie. 2013. "Study Looks at Particles Used in Food." *New York Times.* February 5. Accessed 2018. http://www.nytimes.com/2013/02/06/business/nanoparticles-in-food-raise-concern-by-advocacy-group.html?_r=3&.

TruValue Labs. 2017. "10 studies that show how and why ESG investing works." *Lipper Alpha Insight.* July 10. Accessed 2018. https://lipperalpha.refinitiv.com/2017/07/10-studies-that-show-how-and-why-esg-investing-works.

United Nations. 2015. "Resources." *Sustainable Development Goals* Knowledge Platform. Accessed 2018. https://sustainabledevelopment.un.org/resourcelibrary.

US SIF. 2016. *2016 Report on US Sustainable, Responsible and Impact Investing Trends.* Washington, DC: US SIF Foundation.

US SIF. 2018. *2018 Report On US Sustainable, Responsible And Impact Investing Trends.* Washington, DC: US SIF Foundation.

US SIF and Bloomberg. 2018. *Sustainable, Responsible and Impact Mutual Fund and ETF Chart.* Accessed 2018. https://charts.ussif.org/mfpc/.

US SIF Foundation. 2018. *Report on US Sustainable, Responsible and Impact Investing Trends.* Accessed 2018. https://www.ussif.org/trends.

Wesley Center for Applied Theology. 1999. "The Sermons of John Wesley - Sermon 50, The Use of Money." *Wesley Center Online.* Accessed 2018. http://wesley.nnu.edu/ john-wesley/the-sermons-of-john-wesley-1872-edition/sermon-50-the-use-of-money/.

Worth Rises. 2019. *The Prison Industrial Complex: Mapping Private Sector Players.* April. Accessed 2019. https://worthrises.org/picreport2019.

ACKNOWLEDGMENTS

I would like to thank my strong circle of family and friends who encouraged me throughout this project, especially my wife, Amber. I am deeply appreciative of the power it takes to hold space in the way that you can. Without you, none of this would have ever happened.

I express my thanks to the people and organizations who have provided instrumental assistance throughout the formation of this book:

I am grateful to my editor and creative collaborator, Sable Knapp of Connecting Wild Notions, for her continuous support and motivation for the project. During those times of doubt, you helped me focus and kept this project moving ahead. I would like to thank Heidi Ragsdale of Text Perfected for her valued work readying this book for publication. Thank you, Andrea Domingo of Amy Domingo Art + Design for skillfully formatting the book and creating the cover design. A special thanks to my colleague, friend, and partner, Brad Davis. You helped keep the business running, the encouragement flowing, and maintained trust and faith in my mission. Also, a thank you to Dennis Henderson, friend and one of the smartest, classiest men I know, for his help and support.

Thank you to all the organizations and groups that took the time to speak with me and contributed to the book with their insight and knowledge on the topic of SRI and shareholder advocacy. Thank you, Jennifer Coombs, for your contributions and feedback. Thank you to the College for

Financial Planning for establishing a great CSRIC™ program that allowed me to take my understanding of this area to the next level. I would like to express gratitude to Danielle Fugere for taking the time to speak with me so I could share the importance and the impact of As You Sow. Thank you, Gabe Rissman and Patrick Reed of Stake for the time you spent with me on the phone. I admire the energy you put into your own project, which is making a direct impact every day.

There are countless others worldwide who have, in one way or another, lead to the creation of this book. Sending love to you to all—the experiences I had growing up, the neighborhood where I was raised, the true friends I had, the bullies that made me run for my life, all the mistakes, the successes, the hard times, the struggles, the failures, and the victories.